REFACTORING IN RUBY

REFACTORING IN RUBY

William C. Wake
Kevin Rutherford

✦✦ Addison-Wesley

Upper Saddle River, NJ • Boston • Indianapolis • San Francisco
New York • Toronto • Montreal • London • Munich • Paris • Madrid
Capetown • Sydney • Tokyo • Singapore • Mexico City

The publisher offers excellent discounts on this book when ordered in quantity for bulk purchases or special sales, which may include electronic versions and/or custom covers and content particular to your business, training goals, marketing focus, and branding interests. For more information, please contact:

> U.S. Corporate and Government Sales
> (800) 382-3419
> corpsales@pearsontechgroup.com

For sales outside the United States, please contact:

> International Sales
> international@pearson.com

Visit us on the Web: www.informit.com/aw

Library of Congress Cataloging-in-Publication Data
Wake, William C., 1960-
  Refactoring in Ruby / William C. Wake, Kevin Rutherford.
    p.   cm.
  Includes bibliographical references and index.
  ISBN 978-0-321-54504-6 (pbk. : alk. paper)
  1. Software refactoring. 2. Ruby (Computer program language) I. Rutherford, Kevin. II. Title.
QA76.76.R42.W345 2009
005.1'17—dc22

                                                                2009032115

ISBN-13: 978-0-321-54504-6
ISBN-10:   0-321-54504-4
Text printed in the United States on recycled paper at RR Donnelley in Crawfordsville, Indiana.
First printing, October 2009

For
Angus James Bramwell Rutherford,
a wee gem

In memory
William B. Wake (1938-2007), Dad
and
Steve Metsker (1958-2008), colleague and friend

Contents

Foreword   xvii
Preface   xix
About the Authors   xxiii

PART I   The Art of Refactoring   1

Chapter 1   A Refactoring Example   3

Sparkline Script   3
Consistency   6
Testability   8
Greedy Methods   8
Greedy Module   9
Comments   10
Whole Objects   11
Feature Envy   12
Uncommunicative Names   14
Derived Values   15
Wabi-Sabi   17
Summing Up   18
What's Next   18

Chapter 2   The Refactoring Cycle   19

What Is Refactoring?   19
Smells Are Problems   20
The Refactoring Cycle   21
When Are We Done?   21
Test-Driven/Behavior-Driven Development   22

Exercise   23
    Exercise 2.1: Simple Design   23
What's Next   23

Chapter 3   Refactoring Step by Step   25

The Refactoring Environment   25
Inside a Refactoring   26
The Generic Refactoring Micro-Process   30
Exercises   33
    Exercise 3.1: Small Steps   33
    Exercise 3.2: Inverse Refactorings   33
What's Next   33

Chapter 4   Refactoring Practice   35

Read Other Books   35
Practice Refactoring   35
Exercises to Try   36
Participate in the Community   37
Exercise   38
    Exercise 4.1: Get to Know the Refactorings   38
What's Next   38

PART II   Code Smells   39

Chapter 5   Measurable Smells   41

Comments   42
Long Method   44
Large Module   46
Long Parameter List   48
Exercises   49
    Exercise 5.1: Comments   49
    Exercise 5.2: Long Method   50
    Exercise 5.3: Large Class   51
    Exercise 5.4: Smells and Refactoring   55
    Exercise 5.5: Triggers   55

Chapter 6   Names   57

Type Embedded in Name   59
Uncommunicative Name   60
Inconsistent Names   61
Exercises   62
    Exercise 6.1: Names   62
    Exercise 6.2: Critique the Names   62
    Exercise 6.3: Superclasses   63
    Exercise 6.4: Method Names   63

Chapter 7   Unnecessary Complexity   65

Dead Code   66
Speculative Generality   68
Greedy Method   70
Procedural Code   72
Dynamic Code Creation   74
Exercises   76
    Exercise 7.1: Dead Code (Challenging)   76
    Exercise 7.2: Today versus Tomorrow   76
    Exercise 7.3: Extraction Trade-Offs   77
    Exercise 7.4: Formatting Names   77
    Exercise 7.4: Procedural Code   78

Chapter 8   Duplication   79

Derived Value   80
Repeated Value   81
Duplicated Code   83
Alternative Modules with Different Interfaces   85
Exercises   86
    Exercise 8.1: Rakefile   86
    Exercise 8.2: Two Libraries (Challenging)   86
    Exercise 8.3: Environment Variables   87
    Exercise 8.4: Template   88
    Exercise 8.5: Duplicate Observed Data (Challenging)   89
    Exercise 8.6: Ruby Libraries   90
    Exercise 8.7: Points   90
    Exercise 8.8: XML Report   91

Chapter 9   Conditional Logic   93

Nil Check   94
Special Case   96
Complicated Boolean Expression   98
Control Coupling   100
Simulated Polymorphism   101
Exercises   103
    Exercise 9.1: Null Object   103
    Exercise 9.2: Conditional Expression   103
    Exercise 9.3: Case Statement   104
    Exercise 9.4: Guard Clauses (Challenging)   104
    Exercise 9.5: Factory Method (Challenging)   105

Chapter 10   Data   107

Open Secret   108
Data Class   110
Data Clump   112
Temporary Field   114
Exercises   115
    Exercise 10.1: Alternative Representations   115
    Exercise 10.2: Primitives and Middle Men   115
    Exercise 10.3: Rails Accounts   115
    Exercise 10.4: Long Parameter List   118
    Exercise 10.5: A Counter-Argument   118
    Exercise 10.6: Editor   118
    Exercise 10.7: Library Classes   119
    Exercise 10.8: Hidden State   119
    Exercise 10.9: Proper Names   120
    Exercise 10.10: Checkpoints   122

Chapter 11   Inheritance   125

Implementation Inheritance   126
Refused Bequest   128
Inappropriate Intimacy (Subclass Form)   130
Lazy Class   131
Exercises   133
    Exercise 11.1: ArrayQueue   133
    Exercise 11.2: Relationships   133

Exercise 11.3: Read-Only Documents (Challenging)   134
Exercise 11.4: Inheritance Survey (Challenging)   134

Chapter 12   Responsibility   135

Feature Envy   136
Utility Function   138
Global Variable   140
Inappropriate Intimacy (General Form)   141
Message Chain   143
Middle Man   145
Greedy Module   146
Exercises   148
    Exercise 12.1: Feature Envy   148
    Exercise 12.2: Walking a List   148
    Exercise 12.3: Middle Man   149
    Exercise 12.4: Cart (Challenging)   150
    Exercise 12.5: Utility Functions   151
    Exercise 12.6: Attributes   151
    Exercise 12.7: Message Chains   152

Chapter 13   Accommodating Change   153

Divergent Change   154
Shotgun Surgery   156
Parallel Inheritance Hierarchies   158
Combinatorial Explosion   159
Exercises   160
    Exercise 13.1: CSV Writer   160
    Exercise 13.2: Shotgun Surgery   162
    Exercise 13.3: Hierarchies in Rails   162
    Exercise 13.4: Documents   162

Chapter 14   Libraries   163

Incomplete Library Module   164
Reinvented Wheel   166
Runaway Dependencies   167
Exercises   168
    Exercise 14.1: Layers (Challenging)   168
    Exercise 14.2: Closed Classes (Challenging)   168
    Exercise 14.3: A Missing Function   169

PART III   Programs to Refactor   171

Chapter 15   A Simple Game   173

Code   173
Refactoring   175
    Exercise 15.1: Smells   175
    Exercise 15.2: Easy Changes   175
    Exercise 15.3: Fuse Loops   176
    Exercise 15.4: Result   177
    Exercise 15.5: Next   177
    Exercise 15.6: Constants   177
    Exercise 15.7: Checking for Wins   178
    Exercise 15.8: Representations   178
    Exercise 15.9: Refactoring   179
    Exercise 15.10: Winning Combinations   179
    Exercise 15.11: Iterator   179
Development Episodes   180
    Exercise 15.12: Scores   180
    Exercise 15.13: Comparing Moves   180
    Exercise 15.14: Depth   181
    Exercise 15.15: Caching   181
    Exercise 15.16: Balance   182
    Exercise 15.17: New Features   182
    Exercise 15.18: Min-Max   182
    Exercise 15.19: Do-Over?   182

Chapter 16 Time Recording   183

    Exercise 16.1: Rewrite or Refactor?   187
Preparing the Soil   187
    Exercise 16.2: Project Kick-Off   187
    Exercise 16.3: Test Coverage   188
    Exercise 16.4: Application Object   188
    Exercise 16.5: Testable Methods   189
    Exercise 16.6: Rates of Change   189
    Exercise 16.7: Open Secrets   190
    Exercise 16.8: Hexagonal Architecture (Challenging)   190
Substitute Algorithm   191
    Exercise 16.9: Data Smells   191
    Exercise 16.10: Extending the Database   191

Exercise 16.11: Adapter Tests (Challenging)   192
Exercise 16.12: Database Technology   192
Exercise 16.13: Database Tests (Challenging)   193
Exercise 16.14: Database Adapter (Challenging)   193
Exercise 16.15: Integration Test   194
Exercise 16.16: Going Live   194
Optional Extras   194
Exercise 16.17: Active Record (Challenging)   194
Exercise 16.18: Test-Driven Development   195

Chapter 17   Calculator   197

Exercise 17.1: Smells   198
Code   198
Refactoring   209
Exercise 17.2: Clean Up Calculator   210
Exercise 17.3: Staighten Out is_calculated   210
Exercise 17.4: Controller   210
Exercise 17.5: Generic Calculator   211
Exercise 17.6: UI Class   211
Exercise 17.7: Value and Dimension   211
Exercise 17.8: What Else?   211
Thank You   211

PART IV   Appendices   213

Appendix A   Answers to Selected Questions   215

The Refactoring Cycle   215
Exercise 2.1: Simple Design   215
Refactoring Step by Step   216
Exercise 3.1: Small Steps   216
Exercise 3.2: Inverse Refactorings   216
Refactoring Practice   216
Exercise 4.1: Get to Know the Refactorings   216
Measurable Smells   217
Exercise 5.1: Comments   217
Exercise 5.2: Long Method   217
Exercise 5.3: Large Class   218

Exercise 5.4: Smells and Refactorings   220
Exercise 5.5: Triggers   220
Names   220
Exercise 6.1: Names   220
Exercise 6.2: Critique the Names   221
Exercise 6.3: Superclasses   221
Exercise 6.4: Method Names   221
Unnecessary Complexity   222
Exercise 7.2: Today versus Tomorrow   222
Exercise 7.3: Extraction Trade-Offs   222
Exercise 7.4: Formatting Names   223
Exercise 7.5: Procedural Code   223
Duplication   225
Exercise 8.1: Rakefile   225
Exercise 8.2: Two Libraries   225
Exercise 8.3: Environment Variables   226
Exercise 8.4: Template   227
Exercise 8.5: Duplicate Observed Data   227
Exercise 8.6: Ruby Libraries   228
Exercise 8.7: Points   229
Exercise 8.8: XML Report   229
Conditional Logic   230
Exercise 9.1: Null Object   230
Exercise 9.2: Conditional Expression   230
Exercise 9.3: Case Statement   231
Exercise 9.5: Factory Method   232
Data   233
Exercise 10.1: Alternative Representations   233
Exercise 10.2: Primitives and Middle Men   234
Exercise 10.3: Rails Accounts   234
Exercise 10.4: Long Parameter List   235
Exercise 10.5: A Counter-Argument   235
Exercise 10.6: Editor   235
Exercise 10.7: Library Classes   236
Exercise 10.8: Hidden State   236
Exercise 10.9: Proper Names   236
Exercise 10.10: Checkpoints   237
Inheritance   237
Exercise 11.1: ArrayQueue   237
Exercise 11.2: Relationships   237
Exercise 11.3: Read-Only Documents   237

Contents

Responsibility   239
    Exercise 12.1: Feature Envy   239
    Exercise 12.2: Walking a List   239
    Exercise 12.3: Middle Man   240
    Exercise 12.4: Cart   240
    Exercise 12.5: Utility Functions   240
    Exercise 12.6: Attributes   241
    Exercise 12.7: Message Chains   241
Accommodating Change   241
    Exercise 13.1: CSV Writer   241
    Exercise 13.3: Hierarchies in Rails   243
    Exercise 13.4: Documents   243
Libraries   244
    Exercise 14.1: Layers   244
    Exercise 14.2: Closed Classes   245
    Exercise 14.3: Missing Function   245
A Simple Game   246
    Exercise 15.1: Smells   246
    Exercise 15.3: Fuse Loops   246
    Exercise 15.4: Result   246
    Exercise 15.6: Constants   246
    Exercise 15.8: Representations   246
Time Recording   247
    Exercise 16.1: Rewrite or Refactor?   247
    Exercise 16.3: Test Coverage   248
    Exercise 16.6: Rates of Change   248
    Exercise 16.8: Hexagonal Architecture   248
    Exercise 16.9: Data Smells   248
    Exercise 16.10: Extending the Database   249
    Exercise 16.12: Database Technology   249

Appendix B   Ruby Refactoring Tools   251

Code Smell Detectors   251
Environments with Refactoring Support   252

Bibliography   253
Index   255

Foreword

I want to give you two reasons to work through this book. The first reason is about *right now*, and the second is about *forevermore*.

The reason you need to work through this book *right now* is, well, us: You and me and all the other Ruby programmers out there. While Ruby's a language that, as the saying goes, makes simple things simple and hard things possible, and while we Ruby programmers are intelligent, virtuous, good-looking, kind to animals, and great fun at parties—we're still human. As such, what we make is often awkward, even if it's Ruby code.

So there's this vast and ever-growing sea of Ruby programmers out there, writing awkward Ruby code. I bet you're working on some of that code now, and I'm sure you'll be working on more of it soon. Do you want to be happy doing that? Or sad?

In the past ten years or so, we've learned that a wonderful way to be happy working on code is to *refactor* it as you go. Refactoring means that you change the code to be less awkward on the inside without changing what it does. It's something you can do in small, safe steps while adding features or fixing bugs. As you do, the code keeps getting more pleasant, so your life does too.

Before I give you the second reason to work through the book, I want to share my deepest fear: that you'll only read it, not work through it. That would be a horrible mistake. When I think of you doing that, I imagine all the wonderful tricks in the book entering your head through your eyes—and then far, far too many of them sliding right out of your ears, never to be recalled again. What tricks you do remember will be shuffled off to that part of the brain marked "For Rational Use Only," to be taken out rarely, on special occasions. Mere reading will not make you an expert.

You see, expert behavior is often a-rational. Experts typically *act appropriately* without needing to think through a problem. Indeed, experts often have difficulty explaining why a particular action was appropriate. That's because "thinking through a problem" is expensive, so the brain prefers more efficient routes to correct behavior. Those routes are created through repetition—like by doing the exercises in this book. (Gary Klein's *Sources of Power* is a good book about expert behavior, and Read Montague's *Why Choose This Book?* explains why the brain avoids what we think of as problem-solving.)

When it comes to the awkwardness this book teaches you how to correct, efficient thinking and automatic behavior are important. To get good at this stuff, it's not enough to be able to search for awkwardness—it has to leap out at you as you travel the code. Indeed, I'm happy that Kevin and Bill—like most who write about refactoring—describe awkwardness as "code smells." That's because smell is probably the most powerful, primitive, and least controllable of senses. When you open up a container and the smell of rotting meat hits your brain, you *move*. You act. The smell of rotting code should do the same, but it will only do so after practice blazes well-worn trails through your brain.

So: DO THE EXERCISES.

The reason this book will be valuable to you *forevermore* is that computers are strikingly unsuited to most problems that need solving. They pigheadedly insist that we squeeze every last drop of ambiguity out of a world that's flooded with it. That's a ridiculous … impossible … *inhuman* demand that we put up with only because computers are so *fast*. As a result of this fundamental mismatch—this requirement that we *make up* precision—it takes us a long time to craft a program that works well in the world.

The humble and effective way to arrive at such a program is to put a fledgling version out into the world, watch what happens, and then reshape it (the program, not the world—although people try that too) to make the mismatch less awkward. (And then do it again, and again.) That's an intellectual adventure, especially when you spot concepts implicit in the code that no one's ever quite recognized before, concepts that suddenly open up vast new possibilities and require only a few … well, maybe more than a few … minor … well, maybe not so minor … changes.

Without refactoring, and the style it promotes and supports, the changes the program needs will be too daunting too often. With it, you need nevermore look at a program with that familiar sense of hopeless dread.

And won't that be nice?

—*Brian Marick*
July 4, 2009

Preface

I work mostly as an agile/XP/TDD coach, mostly working with teams developing C++ or C# or Java applications, mostly for Microsoft Windows platforms. Early in any engagement I will inevitably recommend that everyone on the team work through William Wake's *Refactoring Workbook* [26], which I consider to be far and away the best book for any developer who wants to learn to write great code. A short while later in every engagement—and having a UNIX background myself—I urge everyone on the team to improve their project automation skills by adopting a scripting language. I always recommend Ruby because it's easy to learn and object-oriented, and I generally recommend new teams to read Brian Marick's *Everyday Scripting with Ruby* [20] as a starter.

Finally, one day in the summer of 2007, it dawned on me that there was one great book that I couldn't recommend, one that would combine those two facets of all of my projects, but one that hadn't yet been written—a *Refactoring Workbook* for Ruby. So I contacted Bill Wake and suggested we write one, and you're now reading the result.

Compared with Bill's original Java *Refactoring Workbook,* this Ruby edition has a similar overall structure but is otherwise a substantial rewrite. We have retained the core smells, added a few more, and reworked them to apply to Ruby's more dynamic environment. We have replaced all of the code samples, and replaced or revised all of the exercises. We have also rewritten much of the introductory material, principally to reflect the rise in importance of test-driven development during the last five years.

In short, we have tried to create a stand-alone Ruby refactoring workbook for the modern developer, and not a Java book with Ruby code samples. I hope we've come reasonably close to that goal.

—*Kevin Rutherford*
Summer 2009

What Is This Book About?

Refactoring is the art of *improving the design of existing code* and was introduced to the world by Martin Fowler in *Refactoring* [14]. Fowler's book provides dozens of detailed mechanical recipes, each of which describes the steps needed to change one (usually small) aspect of a program's design without breaking anything or changing any behavior.

But to be skilled in refactoring is to be skilled not only in safely and gradually chang-ing code's design, but also in first recognizing where code needs improvement. The agile community has adopted the term *code smell* to describe the anti-patterns in software design, the places where refactoring is needed.

The aim of this book, then, is to help you practice recognizing the smells in exist-ing Ruby code and apply the most important refactoring techniques to eliminate those smells. It will also help you think about how to design code well and to experience the joy of writing great code.

To a lesser extent this book is also a reference work, providing a checklist to help you review for smells in any Ruby code. We have also described the code smells using a standard format; for each smell we describe

- What to Look For: cues that help you spot it
- Why This Is a Problem: the undesirable consequences of having code with this smell
- When to Leave It: the trade-offs that may reduce the priority of fixing it
- How It Got This Way: notes on how it happened
- What to Do: refactorings to remove the smell
- What to Look for Next: what you may see when the smell has been removed

This should help keep the smell pages useful for reference even when you've finished the challenges.

This book does not attempt to catalog or describe the mechanics of refactorings in Ruby. For a comprehensive step-by-step guide to Ruby refactoring recipes, we recommend *Refactoring, Ruby Edition,* by Jay Fields, Shane Harvie, and Martin Fowler [11], which is a Ruby reworking of Fowler's *Refactoring.* It is also not our intention to describe smells in tests; these are already covered well by Gerard Meszaros in *XUnit Test Patterns* [22].

Who Is This Book For?

This book is intended for practicing programmers who write and maintain Ruby code and who want to improve their code's "habitability." We have tried to focus primarily on the universal principles of good design, rather than the details of advanced Ruby-*fu.* Nevertheless, we do expect you to be familiar with most aspects of the Ruby language, the core classes, and the standard libraries. For some exercises you will also need an ex-isting body of Ruby code on hand; usually this will be from your own projects, but you could also use open source code in gems or downloaded applications. Familiarity with refactoring tools or specific IDEs is not assumed (but the examples in this book will provide great help if you wish to practice using such tools).

As mentioned above, it will be helpful to have Fields et al., *Refactoring, Ruby Edition* [11], handy as you work through the exercises. In addition to the mechanics of refactorings, we frequently refer to design patterns, particularly those cataloged by Gamma et al. [16]; you may also find it useful to have available a copy of Russ Olsen's *Design Patterns in Ruby* [24].

What's in This Book?

This book is organized into three sections.

Part I, "The Art of Refactoring," provides an overview of the art of refactoring. We begin with an example; Chapter 1, "A Refactoring Example," takes a small Ruby script containing some common smells and refactors it toward a better design. Chapter 2, "The Refactoring Cycle," takes a brief look at the process of refactoring—when and how to refactor with both legacy code and during test-driven development—while Chapter 3, "Refactoring Step by Step," looks in detail at the tools used and steps taken in a single refactoring. Finally, Chapter 4, "Refactoring Practice," suggests some exercises that you can apply in your own work and provides suggestions for further reading.

Part II, "Code Smells," is the heart of the book, focusing on Ruby code smells. Each chapter here consists of descriptions of a few major code smells, followed by a number of exercises for you to work through. The challenges vary; some ask you to analyze code, others to assess a situation, others to revise code. Not all challenges are equally easy. The harder ones are marked "Challenging"; you'll see that these often have room for variation in their answers. Some exercises have solutions (or ideas to help you find solutions) in Appendix A, "Answers to Selected Questions." Where an exercise relies on Ruby source code you can download it from www.refactoringinruby.info.

Part III, "Programs to Refactor," provides a few "large" programs to help you practice refactoring in a variety of domains.

Part IV, "Appendices," provides selected answers to exercises and brief descriptions of currently available Ruby refactoring tools.

How to Use This Book

This is a *workbook:* Its main purpose is to help you understand the art of refactoring by practicing, with our guidance. There's an easy way to do the exercises: Read the exercise, look up our solution, and nod because it sounds plausible. This may lead you to many insights. Then there's a harder but far better way to do the exercises: Read the exercise, solve the problem, and only then look up our solution. This has a much better chance of leading you to your own insights. Solving a problem is more challenging than merely recognizing a solution and is ultimately much more rewarding.

As you work through the problems, you'll probably find that you disagree with us on some answers. If so, please participate in the community and discuss your opinions with others. That will be more fun for all of us than if you just look at our answers and nod. See Chapter 4, "Refactoring Practice," to learn how to join the discussion.

We think it's more fun to work with others (either with a pair-partner or in a small group), but we recognize this isn't always possible.

Almost all of the code examples need to be done at a computer. Looking for problems, and figuring out how to solve them, is different when you're looking at a program in your environment. Hands-on practice will help you learn more, particularly where you're asked to modify code. Refactoring is a skill that requires practice.

Good luck!

Acknowledgments

Brian Marick has been a huge supporter of the original *Refactoring Workbook* project, and an inspiration with his writing and teaching.

We'd like to thank our core reviewers: Pat Eyler, Micah Martin, Russ Olsen, and Dean Wampler. Their encouragement and suggestions really helped us along the way.

Our involvement in this writing project has placed demands and strains on our families, and we both thank them deeply for their endless patience and support.

Kevin thanks the many people who read drafts of various chapters and provided reactions and feedback, notably Lindsay McEwan; and many thanks to Ashley Moran for pushing the development of Reek, and for introducing lambdas into the Robot tests.

Bill thanks his friends Tom Kubit and Kevin Bradtke for being sounding boards on agile software and other ideas. (Tom gets a double nod for his reviews and discussion of the earlier book.)

Finally, thanks to Chris Guzikowski, Chris Zahn, Raina Chrobak, Kelli Brooks, Julie Nahil, and the others at Pearson who have helped us pull this together.

Contact Us

Feel free to contact us:

Kevin: kevin@rutherford-software.com
          http://www.kevinrutherford.co.uk
Bill: william.wake@acm.org
          http://xp123.com

About the Authors

William C. Wake is a senior consultant with Industrial Logic, Inc. From 2007 to early 2009, he managed development at Gene Codes Forensics, Inc., a producer of bioinformatics software. From 2001 through 2006, he was an independent consultant focused on agile software. He's the author of the *Refactoring Workbook* (Addison-Wesley, 2004) and coauthor of *Design Patterns in Java* (Addison-Wesley, 2006). His web site is www.xp123.com.

Kevin Rutherford, Ph.D., is an independent agile and TDD coach based in the United Kingdom. He has worked in software development for more than 25 years, and since 1997 has been coaching organizations to become highly responsive service providers. He founded the U.K.'s AgileNorth group and is regularly involved on the agile conference circuit. His working practices focus on use of the Theory of Constraints and code quality, and he is the author of the Reek tool for Ruby. His web site is www.kevinrutherford.co.uk.

PART I
The Art of Refactoring

CHAPTER 1

A Refactoring Example

Rather than start with a lot of explanation, we'll begin with a quick example of refactoring to show how you can identify problems in code and systematically clean them up. We'll work "at speed" so you can get the feel of a real session. In later chapters, we'll touch on theory, provide deeper dives into problems and how you fix them, and explore moderately large examples that you can practice on.

Sparkline Script

Let's take a look at a little Ruby script Kevin wrote a while back. The script generates a *sparkline* (a small graph used to display trends, without detail) and does it by generating an SVG document to describe the graphic. (See Figure 1.1.)

The original script was written quickly to display a single sparkline to demonstrate the trends that occur when tossing a coin. It was never intended to live beyond that single use, but then someone asked Kevin to generalize it so that the code could be used to create other sparklines and other SVG documents. The code needs to become more reusable and maintainable, which means we'd better get it into shape.

Figure 1.1 A sparkline

Here's the original code:

```
NUMBER_OF_TOSSES = 1000
BORDER_WIDTH = 50

def toss
  2 * (rand(2)*2 - 1)
end

def values(n)
  a = [0]
  n.times { a << (toss + a[-1]) }
  a
end

def spark(centre_x, centre_y, value)
  "<rect x=\"#{centre_x-2}\" y=\"#{centre_y-2}\"
    width=\"4\" height=\"4\"
    fill=\"red\" stroke=\"none\" stroke-width=\"0\" />
  <text x=\"#{centre_x+6}\" y=\"#{centre_y+4}\"
    font-family=\"Verdana\" font-size=\"9\"
    fill=\"red\" >#{value}</text>"
end

$tosses = values(NUMBER_OF_TOSSES)
points = []
$tosses.each_index { |i| points << "#{i},#{200-$tosses[i]}" }

data = "<svg xmlns=\"http://www.w3.org/2000/svg\"
    xmlns:xlink=\"http://www.w3.org/1999/xlink\" >
  <!-- x-axis -->
  <line x1=\"0\" y1=\"200\" x2=\"#{NUMBER_OF_TOSSES}\" y2=\"200\"
          stroke=\"#999\" stroke-width=\"1\" />
  <polyline fill=\"none\" stroke=\"#333\" stroke-width=\"1\"
    points = \"#{points.join(' ')}\" />
  #{spark(NUMBER_OF_TOSSES-1, 200-$tosses[-1], $tosses[-1])}
</svg>"

puts "Content-Type: image/svg+xml
Content-Length: #{data.length}

#{data}"
```

Forty lines of code, and what a mess! Before we dive in and change things, take a moment to review the script. Which aspects of it strike you as convoluted, or unreadable, or even unmaintainable? Part II, "Code Smells," of this book lists over forty common code problems: Each kind of problem is known as a *code smell*, and each has very specific characteristics, consequences, and remedies. For the purposes of this quick refactoring demonstration, we'll use the names of these smells (so that you can cross-reference with Part II, "Code Smells," if you wish), but otherwise we just want to get on with fixing the code. Here are the more obvious problems we noticed in the code:

- **Comments:** There's a comment in the SVG document (line 29). As a comment in the SVG output that's not a bad thing, because the SVG is quite opaque. But it also serves to comment the Ruby script, which suggests that the string is too complex.

- **Inconsistent Style:** Part of the SVG document is broken out into a separate method (line 34), whereas most is built inline in the `data` string.

- **Long Parameter List:** Strictly speaking, the list of properties of the XML elements aren't Ruby parameters. But they are long lists, and we feel sure they will cause problems later.

- **Uncommunicative Name:** The code uses `data` as the name of the SVG document, `i` as an iterator index (line 25), `a` as the name of an array (line 9), and `n` as the number of array elements (line 8).

- **Dead Code:** The constant `BORDER_WIDTH` (line 2) is unused.

- **Greedy Method:** `toss` tosses a coin and also scales it to be −2 or +2.

- **Derived Value:** Most of the numbers representing SVG coordinates and shape sizes could probably be derived from the number of tosses and the sparkline's max and min values.

- **Duplicated Code:** The text markers for the start and end tags of XML elements are repeated throughout the code; the calculation `200-tosses[x]` is repeated (lines 25, 34).

- **Data Clump:** The SVG components' parameters include several x-y pairs that represent points on the display canvas (lines 15, 18, 30). Some have further parameters that go to make up a rectangle (lines 16, 30). Strictly, these are parameters to SVG elements, and this is therefore a problem in the definition of SVG.

- **Global Variable:** Why is `tosses` a global variable at all?

- **Utility Function:** One might argue that all of the methods here (lines 4, 8, 14) are Utility Functions.

- **Greedy Module:** The script isn't a class, as such, but it does have multiple responsibilities: Some of the script deals with tossing coins, some deals with drawing pictures, and some wraps the SVG document in an HTTP message.

- **Divergent Change:** The `data` string (lines 27–35) is probably going to need to be different for almost every imaginable variation on this script.

- **Reinvented Wheel:** There are already Ruby libraries for manipulating XML elements, and even for creating SVG documents.

Which should we address first? When faced with a long to-do list of code smells it's easy to feel a little intimidated. It's important to remember at this stage that we can't fix everything in one sitting; we'll have to proceed in small, safe steps. We also want to avoid planning too far ahead—the code will change with every step, and right now it would be a futile waste of energy to attempt to visualize what the code might be like even a few minutes from now.

So in the next few sections we're simply going to address the smells that strike us as "next" on the to-do list, without regard to what "next" might mean, or to what will happen after that. It is entirely likely that you would address the smells in a different order, and that's just fine; experience suggests that we're likely to finish up at approximately the same place later.

First, let's tidy up a little.

Consistency

We can easily remove the **Dead Code** and change the **Global Variable**; at the same time we'll create a simple method for each SVG element type we use, and convert those quoted strings too:

```
NUMBER_OF_TOSSES = 1000

def toss
  2 * (rand(2)*2 - 1)
end

def values(n)
  a = [0]
  n.times { a << (toss + a[-1]) }
  a
end

def rect(centre_x, centre_y)
  %Q{<rect x="#{centre_x-2}" y="#{centre_y-2}"
    width="4" height="4"
    fill="red" stroke="none"  stroke-width="0" />"}
end
```

```
def text(x, y, msg)
  %Q{<text x="#{x}" y="#{y}"
    font-family="Verdana" font-size="9"
      fill="red" >#{msg}</text>"}
end

def line(x1, y1, x2, y2)
  %Q{<line x1="#{x1}" y1="#{y1}" x2="#{x2}" y2="#{y2}"
    stroke="#999" stroke-width="1" />}
end

def polyline(points)
  %Q{<polyline fill="none" stroke="#333" stroke-width="1"
    points = "#{points.join(' ')}" />"}
end

def spark(centre_x, centre_y, value)
  "#{rect(centre_x, centre_y)}
    #{text(centre_x+6, centre_y+4, value)}"
end

tosses = values(NUMBER_OF_TOSSES)
points = []
tosses.each_index { |i| points << "#{i},#{200-tosses[i]}" }

data = %Q{<svg xmlns="http://www.w3.org/2000/svg"
    xmlns:xlink="http://www.w3.org/1999/xlink" >
  <!-- x-axis -->
  #{line(0, 200, NUMBER_OF_TOSSES, 200)}
  #{polyline(points)}
  #{spark(NUMBER_OF_TOSSES-1, 200-tosses[-1], tosses[-1])}
</svg>}

puts "Content-Type: image/svg+xml
Content-Length: #{data.length}

#{data}"
```

The overall **Greedy Module** is now somewhat more apparent, as we have more methods dealing with SVG elements now. However, note that each of the methods we just added is also a **Greedy Method**, because each knows something about an SVG element and something about how we want the sparkline to look. So we've traded some problems for others, and that's a very subjective process.

Testability

We changed quite a lot of code there, and each time we extracted a method we re-ran the script to make sure we hadn't broken the sparkline. But the HTTP wrapper (lines 52–54) forces us into a particularly unfriendly test environment. So to improve testability, we'll delete that HTTP wrapper and simply replace it with:

```
puts data
```

More on testing as we proceed, but for now that little change makes it easier to run `sparky.rb`.

Greedy Methods

Each of the SVG drawing methods we extracted is greedy, because they know about SVG *and* sparkline formatting. We want to address that next, because those two kinds of knowledge are likely to cause change at different rates in the future.

We'll begin with `rect`: we passed in two parameters from the caller, but to make this method fully independent of the sparklines application we need to pass in 5 more:

```
def rect(centre_x, centre_y, width, height,
         fill, stroke, stroke_width)
  %Q{<rect x="#{centre_x}" y="#{centre_y}"
    width="#{width}" height="#{height}"
    fill="#{fill}" stroke="#{stroke}"
    stroke-width="#{stroke_width}" />}
end
```

This is ugly, but right now it's what the code seems to want. We're trading one smell for another again here, but little bits of flexibility and maintainability are created as by-products.

The caller changes to match:

```
SQUARE_SIDE = 4

def spark(centre_x, centre_y, value)
  "#{rect(centre_x-(SQUARE_SIDE/2), centre_y-(SQUARE_SIDE/2),
        SQUARE_SIDE, SQUARE_SIDE, 'red', 'none', 0)}
    #{text(centre_x+6, centre_y+4, value)}"
end
```

The changes to `spark` made some **Derived Values** apparent, so we also took the opportunity to fix that by introducing a constant for the size of the little red square.

We can now introduce extra parameters to `text`, `line`, and `polyline` in the same way:

```
def text(x, y, msg, font_family, font_size, fill)
  %Q{<text x="#{x}" y="#{y}"
    font-family="#{font_family}" font-size="#{font_size}"
    fill="#{fill}" >#{msg}</text>}
end

def line(x1, y1, x2, y2, stroke, stroke_width)
  %Q{<line x1="#{x1}" y1="#{y1}" x2="#{x2}" y2="#{y2}"
    stroke="#{stroke}" stroke-width="#{stroke_width}" />}
end

def polyline(points, fill, stroke, stroke_width)
  %Q{<polyline fill="#{fill}" stroke="#{stroke}"
    stroke-width="#{stroke_width}"
    points = "#{points.join(' ')}" />}
end
```

The calling code changes to match, for example:

```
SQUARE_SIDE = 4
SPARK_COLOR = 'red'

def spark(centre_x, centre_y, value)
  "#{rect(centre_x-(SQUARE_SIDE/2), centre_y-(SQUARE_SIDE/2),
        SQUARE_SIDE, SQUARE_SIDE, SPARK_COLOR, 'none', 0)}
  #{text(centre_x+6, centre_y+4, value,
        'Verdana', 9, SPARK_COLOR)}"
end
```

Note that we have again traded problems. The four drawing methods are no longer greedy, but now their callers know some SVG magic (color names, font names, and drawing element dimensions). This kind of trading is a completely natural part of refactoring, as we create areas of stability within the code. We'll return to address this **Inappropriate Intimacy (General Form)** later.

Greedy Module

That may not be the last we see of **Greedy Methods**, but code changes in the previous section have highlighted another of the problems in the original code: There's now an even clearer distinction between code that knows how to write an SVG document and code that knows what a sparkline should look like.

To fix that, we're going to extract a module for the SVG methods. We'll put it in a new source file called svg.rb:

```
module SVG
  def self.rect(centre_x, centre_y, width, height, fill,
      stroke, stroke_width)
    %Q{<rect x="#{centre_x}" y="#{centre_y}"
    width="#{width}" height="#{height}"
    fill="#{fill}" stroke="#{stroke}"
    stroke-width="#{stroke_width}" />}
  end

  # etc...
end
```

A quick glance at this module shows that the **Data Clumps** and **Long Parameter Lists** we predicted are now a reality. (And in fact, each of these SVG elements can take more parameters than we have provided here, so the problem is much worse than it seems.) Note also that we haven't yet moved all of the XML into the SVG module, but to do that we'll have to decide how to deal with nested XML elements. We want to make the calling script a little clearer before diving into the design of the SVG interface.

Comments

There's a comment in the SVG document generated by the script:

```
<!-- x-axis -->
```

The comment is there because it's difficult to match the magic SVG words and symbols to the format and structure of a sparkline. We don't like commenting source code, but we have no problem creating a self-documenting SVG document, so we're happy to keep the comment. The problem is that one comment isn't enough; the output SVG needs to have a few more! Worse, the script doesn't communicate the sparkline's structure to us, its readers, and so we could easily break it accidentally in the future. We'll fix both of these issues by extracting a method for each component of the sparkline's structure:

```
def sparkline(points)
  "<!-- sparkline -->
  #{SVG.polyline(points, 'none', '#333', 1)}"
end
```

```
def spark(centre_x, centre_y, value)
  "<!-- spark -->
  #{SVG.rect(centre_x-(SQUARE_SIDE/2), centre_y-(SQUARE_SIDE/2),
            SQUARE_SIDE, SQUARE_SIDE, SPARK_COLOR, 'none', 0)}
  <!-- final value -->
  #{SVG.text(centre_x+6, centre_y+4, value,
            'Verdana', 9, SPARK_COLOR)}"
end

def x_axis(points)
  "<!-- x-axis -->
  #{SVG.line(0, 200, points.length, 200, '#999', 1)}"
end
```

While extracting x_axis we also removed its dependency on the constant NUMBER_
OF_TOSSES. In fact, we now see no reason for the constant to exist; we'll inline it in the
call to values, and recalculate its value in the call to spark:

```
tosses = values(1000)

#...

data = %Q{<svg xmlns="http://www.w3.org/2000/svg"
    xmlns:xlink="http://www.w3.org/1999/xlink" >
  #{x_axis(points)}
  #{sparkline(points)}
  #{spark(tosses.length-1, 200-tosses[-1], tosses[-1])}
</svg>}
```

Whole Objects

Leaving aside the horrors of that last string for a moment, look inside it at the call to spark:
We have a **Long Parameter List** in which every parameter is calculated from tosses.
Let's use Preserve Whole Object by pushing those calculations into the spark method:

```
def spark(y_values)
  final_value = y_values[-1]
  centre_x = y_values.length-1
  centre_y = 200 - final_value
  "<!-- spark -->
  #{SVG.rect(centre_x-(SQUARE_SIDE/2), centre_y-(SQUARE_SIDE/2),
            SQUARE_SIDE, SQUARE_SIDE, SPARK_COLOR, 'none', 0)}
  <!-- final value -->
  #{SVG.text(centre_x+6, centre_y+4, final_value,
            'Verdana', 9, SPARK_COLOR)}"
end
```

`spark`'s parameter could represent coin tosses, stock prices, or temperatures, so we renamed it while we remembered.

Now take another look at x_axis—it only cares how many y-values there are, but it isn't interested in the points. We can pass in the y-values instead:

```
def x_axis(y_values)
  "<!-- x-axis -->
  #{SVG.line(0, 200, y_values.length, 200, '#999', 1)}"
end
```

This means that the only code that cares about `points` is the `sparkline` method. We can move the calculation of `points` into that method:

```
def sparkline(y_values)
  points = []
  y_values.each_index { |i| points << "#{i},#{200-y_values[i]}" }
  "<!-- sparkline -->
  #{SVG.polyline(points, 'none', '#333', 1)}"
end
```

And so finally (and after a little tidying up), the creation of the SVG document looks like this:

```
puts %Q{<svg xmlns="http://www.w3.org/2000/svg"
    xmlns:xlink="http://www.w3.org/1999/xlink" >
      #{x_axis(tosses)}
      #{sparkline(tosses)}
      #{spark(tosses)}
    </svg>}
```

Feature Envy

Look again at that sequence of method calls taking `tosses` as the single parameter. That chunk of code has more affinity with the `tosses` array than it does with the rest of the script. Same goes for the three methods `spark`, `sparkline`, and `x_axis`—they all do more with the array of `y_values` than they do with anything else. There's a missing class here, one whose state is the array, and which has methods that know how to draw the pieces of a sparkline. Instances of this missing class represent sparklines, so finding a name for it is easy. First, we'll create a simple stub to hold the array:

```
class Sparkline
  attr_reader :y_values
```

```
  def initialize(y_values)
    @y_values = y_values
  end

end
```

Then we'll update the final `puts` call to use it:

```
sp = Sparkline.new(values(1000))
puts %Q{<svg xmlns="http://www.w3.org/2000/svg"
     xmlns:xlink="http://www.w3.org/1999/xlink" >
        #{x_axis(sp.y_values)}
        #{sparkline(sp.y_values)}
        #{spark(sp.y_values)}
       </svg>}
```

Now we're going to move the three methods (and that huge string) onto the new class. In real life we would do them one by one, testing as we go; but for the sake of brevity here let's cut to the final state of the new class:

```
class Sparkline

  def initialize(y_values)
    @y_values = y_values
  end

  def to_svg
    %Q{<svg xmlns="http://www.w3.org/2000/svg"
           xmlns:xlink="http://www.w3.org/1999/xlink" >
        #{x_axis}
        #{sparkline}
        #{spark}
       </svg>}
  end

private
  def x_axis
    "<!-- x-axis -->
    #{SVG.line(0, 200, y_values.length, 200, '#999', 1)}"
  end

  def sparkline
    points = []
    y_values.each_index { |i| points << "#{i},#{200-y_values[i]}" }
    "<!-- sparkline -->
    #{SVG.polyline(points, 'none', '#333', 1)}"
  end

  SQUARE_SIDE = 4
  SPARK_COLOR = 'red'
```

```
def spark
  final_value = y_values[-1]
  centre_x = y_values.length-1
  centre_y = 200 - final_value
  "<!-- spark -->
   #{SVG.rect(centre_x-(SQUARE_SIDE/2), centre_y-(SQUARE_SIDE/2),
            SQUARE_SIDE, SQUARE_SIDE, SPARK_COLOR, 'none', 0)}
   <!-- final value -->
   #{SVG.text(centre_x+6, centre_y+4, final_value,
            'Verdana', 9, SPARK_COLOR)}"
end

end
```

Notice that the `attr_reader` for `y_values` is no longer necessary, so we deleted it. The public accessor was needed in the early phases of that refactoring step so that we could introduce the new class without breaking any other code. But after the methods had all migrated into the new class, the array is used only internally, and thus can be hidden.

For completeness, here's what remains of the original script:

```
require 'sparkline'

def toss
  2 * (rand(2)*2 - 1)
end

def values(n)
  a = [0]
  n.times { a << (toss + a[-1]) }
  a
end

puts Sparkline.new(values(1000)).to_svg
```

Uncommunicative Names

Now the script is so short, the **Uncommunicative Names** really stand out. Here's an alternative version with better names for anything we thought wasn't communicating clearly:

```
require 'sparkline'

def zero_or_one() rand(2) end
```

```
def one_or_minus_one
  (zero_or_one * 2) - 1
end

def next_value(y_values)
  y_values[-1] + one_or_minus_one
end

def y_values
  result = [0]
  1000.times { result << next_value(result) }
  result
end

puts Sparkline.new(y_values).to_svg
```

While fixing the names we discovered a 2 being used to scale the sparkline vertically; we removed it in the interest of honest statistics. We find defects often during the course of refactoring. Usually this is because the process of refactoring has revealed something that previously wasn't obvious. It's okay to fix these defects, provided you consciously switch hats for a few moments while doing so.

Derived Values

Now it's time to tackle all those **Derived Values** we noticed right at the outset. They have all migrated into Sparkline, which is nicely convenient. I'll begin with the 200s: The x-axis is drawn halfway down the canvas, at y-coordinate 200, and so every y_value is scaled vertically by 200. (Y-coordinates increase down the page; so point (0, 0) is at the top-left corner and point (0, 200) is 200 drawing units below that.) In fact, 200-y does two things: It translates the line vertically downward by 200 units *and* it flips the line over so that positive y-values appear above negative y-values. These are *transforms* of the image: Reflection followed by translation. SVG (currently) has no reflection transform, but it does offer translation, and we feel we'll get simpler Ruby code if we use it. First, then, we'll invert the sparkline's y-values in the constructor:

```
def initialize(y_values)
  @height_above_x_axis = y_values.max
  @height_below_x_axis = y_values.min
  @final_value = y_values[-1]
  @y_values = reflect_top_and_bottom(y_values)
end

def reflect_top_and_bottom(y_values)
  y_values.map { |y| -y }
end
```

and change `sparkline` and `spark` correspondingly:

```
def sparkline
  points = []
  y_values.each_index { |i| points << "#{i},#{y_values[i] + 200}" }
  "<!-- sparkline -->
    #{SVG.polyline(points, 'none', '#333', 1)}"
end

def spark
  centre_x = y_values.length-1
  centre_y = y_values[-1] + 200
  "<!-- spark -->
    #{SVG.rect(centre_x-(SQUARE_SIDE/2), centre_y-(SQUARE_SIDE/2),
              SQUARE_SIDE, SQUARE_SIDE, SPARK_COLOR, 'none', 0)}
  <!-- final value -->
    #{SVG.text(centre_x+6, centre_y+4, @final_value,
              'Verdana', 9, SPARK_COLOR)}"
end
```

Next, we use an SVG transform to move the whole graphic down the screen by 200 units:

```
def to_svg
  %Q{<svg xmlns="http://www.w3.org/2000/svg"
        xmlns:xlink="http://www.w3.org/1999/xlink" >
    <g transform="translate(0,200)">
      #{x_axis}
      #{sparkline}
      #{spark}
    </g>
  </svg>}
end
```

And now we can remove those magic 200s from the drawing methods. For example, `x_axis` now becomes

```
def x_axis
  "<!-- x-axis -->
    #{SVG.line(0, 0, y_values.length, 0, '#999', 1)}"
end
```

We now have more SVG magic—the `<g>` element—in the code, but also there is less duplication, and we consider that much more important.

We have now removed all but one of the magic 200s; before going any further, we want to document its meaning:

```
def to_svg
  height_above_x_axis = 200
  %Q{<svg xmlns="http://www.w3.org/2000/svg"
        xmlns:xlink="http://www.w3.org/1999/xlink" >
    <g transform="translate(0,#{height_above_x_axis})">
      #{x_axis}
      #{sparkline}
      #{spark}
    </g>
  </svg>}
end
```

It is now clear that the 200 is simply a guess as to what a reasonable value might be. If the sparkline's y-values stray outside of the range −200..200 we'll find the line disappears off the edge of the graphic. We spoke to our customer just now, and he agrees that we should replace the 200 with the maximum y-value:

```
def to_svg
  %Q{<svg xmlns="http://www.w3.org/2000/svg"
        xmlns:xlink="http://www.w3.org/1999/xlink" >
    <g transform="translate(0,#{height_above_x_axis})">
      #{x_axis}
      #{sparkline}
      #{spark}
    </g>
  </svg>}
end

def initialize(y_values)
  @height_above_x_axis = y_values.max
  @final_value = y_values[-1]
  @y_values = reflect_top_and_bottom(y_values)
end
```

Wabi-Sabi

We've made a number of refactoring changes to the code, and in the process its structure has altered a great deal. Have we finished? No, and in a sense we never will. Software can never be perfect, and there's usually little point in chasing down that last scintilla of design perfection. Any code will always be a "work in progress"—the important thing is to have removed the major problems, and to know what slight odors remain.

The title of this section is also the name of the Japanese artistic style that celebrates the incomplete, the unfinished, and the transitory. Try to become used to thinking of your code as a *process* and not simply an *artifact;* aim for *better*, not *best.* Read more in Leonard Koren's *Wabi-Sabi: For Artists, Designers, Poets and Philosophers* [19], for example.

Summing Up

Here's the current state of the main script after the refactorings:

```
require 'sparkline'

def zero_or_one() rand(2) end

def one_or_minus_one
  (zero_or_one * 2) - 1
end

def next_value(y_values)
  y_values[-1] + one_or_minus_one
end

def y_values
  result = [0]
  1000.times { result << next_value(result) }
  result
end

puts Sparkline.new(y_values).to_svg
```

(You can get complete copies of the "before" and "after" states of the code from our download, which you can find online at http://github.com/kevinrutherford/rrwb-code.)

The code still has some smells: sparkline.rb still knows too much about SVG; svg.rb still has long parameter lists; and the functionality of the SVG module duplicates that of a standard Ruby library. Notice also that the code has expanded from 40 lines to 100, and from one source file to three—all without increasing the script's functionality.

Overall, though, the code is much more readable and maintainable than it was before. We have traded size for flexibility, and in the future it will be much easier to reuse any of the various parts of this code. This is a reasonable place to stop for now.

What's Next

Now that we've seen a quick example of how refactoring can improve code, we'll look at how refactoring fits into the development process, and then consider different problems in code and examples of how to address them.

## CHAPTER 2

The Refactoring Cycle

In this chapter, we'll define refactoring and code smells. Then we'll look at the fundamental cycle of how to improve code with refactoring. Rules for simple design will tell us when we've done enough. We'll close with a look at how refactoring is a key part of test-driven development.

What Is Refactoring?

Refactoring is the art of safely improving the design of existing code. In *Refactoring* [14], Martin Fowler describes it thus:

> "Refactoring is the process of changing a software system in such a way that it does not alter the external behavior of the code yet improves its internal structure."

This has a few implications:

- *Refactoring does not include just any changes in a system:* Although refactoring should always be part of the process used to create new code, it's not the part that adds new features. Test-driven development, for example, consists of writing a test, then writing new code to introduce new features, and, finally, refactoring to improve the design.

- *Refactoring is not rewriting from scratch:* Although there are times when it's better to start fresh, refactoring changes the balance point, making it possible to improve code rather than take the risk of rewriting it. Sven Gorts points out (private communication) that refactoring preserves the knowledge embedded in the existing code.

- *Refactoring is not just any restructuring intended to improve code:* Refactorings strive to be *safe* transformations. Even *big* refactorings that change large amounts of code are divided into smaller, safe refactorings. (In the best case, refactorings are so well defined that they can be automated.) We won't regard a change as refactoring if it leaves the code not working (that is, not passing its tests) for longer than a working session.

- *Refactoring supports emergent design:* Refactoring changes the balance point between up-front design and emergent design. Up-front design is design done in advance of implementation; emergent design is design intertwined with implementation. The trade-off between up-front and emergent design hinges on how well we can anticipate problems or assess them in code, and whether it's easier to *design and then translate to code* or to *code and then improve.* Refactoring lowers the cost and risk of the emergent approach. (You might argue about where the line is, but you probably agree that it shifts.)

- *Refactorings can be small or large:* Many refactorings are small. Ideally, small refactorings are applied "mercilessly" enough that large refactorings are rarely needed. Even when applying large-scale refactorings, the approach is not *no new features for six months while we refactor,* but rather, *refactor as we go, and keep the system running at all times.*

Smells Are Problems

Code smells are warning signs about potential problems in code. Not all smells indicate a problem, but most are worthy of a look and a decision.

Some people dislike the term *smell,* and prefer to talk about *potential problems* or *flaws,* but we think smell is a good metaphor. Think about what happens when you open a fridge that has a few things going bad inside. Some smells will be strong, and it will be obvious what to do about them. Other smells will be subtler; you won't be sure if the problem is caused by the leftover peas or last week's milk. Some food in the fridge may be bad without having a particularly bad smell. Code smells are a bit like that: Some are obvious, some aren't. Some mask other problems. Some go away unexpectedly when you fix something else.

Smells usually describe localized problems. It would be nice if people could find problems easily across a whole system. But humans aren't so good at that job; local smells work with our tendency to consider only the part we're looking at right now.

Finally, remember that a smell is an indication of a *potential* problem, not a guarantee of an *actual* problem. You will occasionally find false positives—things that smell to you, but are actually better than the alternatives. But most code has plenty of real smells that can keep you busy.

The Refactoring Cycle

There's a basic pattern for refactoring:

The Refactoring Cycle

start with working, tested code
while the design can be simplified:

>   choose the worst smell

>   select a refactoring that will address the smell

>   apply the refactoring

>   check that the tests still pass

We try to select refactorings that improve the code in each trip through the cycle. Because none of the steps change the program's observable behavior, the program remains in a working state. Thus, the cycle improves code but retains behavior. The trickiest part of the whole process is identifying the smell, and that's why the bulk of this book emphasizes that topic.

Is this approach to refactoring guaranteed to get to the ideal design for a problem? Unfortunately, no, as there's no guarantee that you can reach a global maximum by looking at local properties. But it's easier to get design insights that transform a solution when the code is as clean as possible.

Refactoring is like crossing a stream. One way to cross a stream is to take a running leap and hope for the best. The refactoring way is to find stepping stones and to cross the stream by stepping on one stone at a time; that way, you're less likely to get wet.

When you start refactoring, it's best to start with the easy stuff (for example, breaking up large methods or renaming things for clarity). You'll find that this lets you see and fix the remaining problems more easily.

When Are We Done?

How do we know when to stop refactoring and move on to more development? One approach is to seek the "simplest" design. In *Extreme Programming Explained* [4] Kent Beck identified four rules for simple design:

Simple Design:

1. Passes all the tests.
2. Communicates every intention important to the programmers.
3. Has no duplication of code, or of logic, or of knowledge.
4. Contains no unnecessary code.

If your code violates these rules (which are in priority order), you have a problem to address. A shorthand name for these rules is OAOO, which stands for *once and only once*. The code has to state something once so that it can pass its tests and communicate the programmer's understanding and intent. And it should say things only once—that is, with no duplication.

Another name for the third rule is "Don't Repeat Yourself," or the *DRY principle* [17]. Most of the smells cataloged in Part II, "Code Smells," boil down to duplication of some kind; and spotting it can be quite an art—be wary of hidden duplication, such as parallel class hierarchies, for example. But duplication is occasionally acceptable, where its existence helps the code communicate intent; after all, code will be read many more times than it will be written.

It's hard to clean up code that hasn't been kept clean; few teams can afford to lock the doors for months on a quest for perfection. But we can learn to make our code better during development, and we can add a little energy each time we're working in an area.

Test-Driven/Behavior-Driven Development

Applying refactorings in the midst of a development episode can lead to confusion, unsafe transformations, or, in the worst case, broken code. So it's best to think of *development* and *refactoring* as different: different skills, using different techniques, to be performed at different times in the overall cycle. Think of development and refactoring as different hats—you can only wear one of them at any time.

Test-driven development (TDD) and behavior-driven development (BDD) make the distinction between the two hats very clear. They share the following microprocess:

The TDD/BDD Micro-Process

RED   Write a new test/example and see it fail.
GREEN   Get all tests passing again quickly, using the most naive approach you can see.
REFACTOR   Transition to the simplest design that passes all current tests, by removing any
           smells you just introduced.
(repeat)   Go around again, aiming to be back here every few minutes or so.

The refactoring step is what makes this process *sustainable*. Without it the code would quickly degenerate into the legacy spaghetti you've no doubt seen on many a software development project. Well-factored code is easier to read and more amenable to change; so the small investment in frequent refactoring steps is gradually repaid, with compound interest, as the code grows.

Note that refactoring only occurs on a "green bar"—that is, when all tests are passing. (The tests act as a regression suite, ensuring that we can't break any existing behavior while we're fixing the design.) Typically only a small amount of code will have been changed or introduced in going from RED to GREEN. This is the code to be reviewed for smells, although that review must be done *in the context of the whole of the existing codebase.* To help with this part of the process we have included a code review checklist on the inside covers of this book; we have also developed Reek, a free software tool that warns about smells in Ruby code (see Appendix B, "Ruby Refactoring Tools," for details of this and other related tools).

We both use test-driven development as the core of our development process. Note that the discipline of refactoring doesn't require a test-driven approach, but code created this way will typically have fewer errors and will need less of the big refactoring that other code requires. In particular, the bigger examples in the last half of this book would be much smaller and less smelly if they'd been done using test-driven development.

For a deeper introduction to TDD see the books by Dave Astels [1] and Kent Beck [3]. For more on BDD see David Chelimsky et al.'s *The RSpec Book: Behaviour Driven Development with RSpec, Cucumber, and Friends* [8].

Exercise

> ### Exercise 2.1: Simple Design
>
> A. Justify each of Beck's rules for simple design.
>
> B. Why are these rules in priority order? Can you find an example where communication overrides avoidance of duplication?
>
> *See page 215 for solution ideas.*

What's Next

That was a look at how refactoring fits into the overall process(es) of software development. Next we'll dive deep into what makes a single refactoring work, and the environmental conditions that will help you do it safely.

CHAPTER 3

Refactoring Step by Step

It's time we looked in detail at the mechanics of refactoring. In this chapter we'll work through the steps involved in *Hide Delegate;* but first we need to review our tools.

The Refactoring Environment

Refactoring can be done on any code at any time, but it's easier and safer with a supportive environment. Be sure to have most of the following tools ready at your side before you begin refactoring:

- *Team or Partner:* For nontrivial decisions about code, it's helpful to have more than one person considering the problem. A team can often generate ideas better than one person alone: Different people have different experiences and different exposure to different parts of the system.

- *Tests:* Even though refactorings are designed to be safe, it's possible to make a mistake while applying them. By having a test suite that is run before and after refactoring, you help ensure that you change the design of your code, not its effects.

"If you want to refactor, the essential precondition is having solid tests."

—Martin Fowler, *Refactoring* [14]

This is even more true for Ruby than it was when Fowler wrote it about refactoring in Java. Because in Ruby there's no *compile* step: The only way to find out whether our code still works is to run it.

What if you don't have tests? Then add them, at least to the areas affected by the refactoring. Sometimes this is tricky—you may be unable to test effectively without changing the design, and yet it's unsafe to change the design without tests. (If you find yourself in this position, you may find the techniques in Michael Feathers' *Working Effectively with Legacy Code* [10] helpful.) And note, by the way, that areas that are tricky to test often indicate other problems in the design.

- *Testing Framework:* `Test::Unit` is installed as part of the standard Ruby distribution, and `rspec` is available as a gem. It can also be very handy to have `autotest` run your tests while you work.

  We have provided tests or `rspec` examples for most of the code samples used in the exercises; you'll find them in the download. Get into the habit of running them as you review the code in each exercise.

- *CRC (Class, Responsibilities, Collaborators) Cards or UML Sketches:* Refactoring is design. Sometimes you may hold a CRC card session or draw Unified Modeling Language (UML) sketches to compare alternative strategies, particularly when moving responsibilities around among classes or modules. (For more detail on the CRC card approach, see Kent Beck and Ward Cunningham's article "A Laboratory For Teaching Object-Oriented Thinking" [5]).

- *Configuration Management/Version Control:* If you make a mistake while refactoring, you'd like to have the option to return to the last known good point. Alternatively, you may want to apply a refactoring, but you may not be sure if the result will be an improvement; it can be helpful to have the option to try it and then decide whether to keep the result. Either way, it's worth getting into the habit of committing your code frequently (every time the tests all pass), and it's worth making sure you have a version control system that lets you do this.

- *Sophisticated Integrated Development Environment (IDE):* A few Ruby environments now have growing support for automated refactoring tools (see Appendix B, "Ruby Refactoring Tools," for details of some of these). Tools can remove a lot of the error-prone tedium of refactoring. But most refactorings have no tool support, and even with automation you still have to decide which refactoring to apply.

Inside a Refactoring

One of the defining aspects of refactoring is the focus on safe transformations. We'll walk through a simple refactoring. Along the way we'll derive some guidelines that will help us better understand how refactorings work.

Consider the refactoring *Hide Delegate*. Its goal is to encapsulate the path to an object, so that clients are decoupled from the implementation details of how to reach it.

Imagine we have

```
class Rectangle
  attr_reader :top_left, :width, :height
end

class Point
  attr_reader :x, :y
end
```

Any client code wishing to find the *x*-coordinate of a rectangle's left edge will have code fragments such as `rect.top_left.x`, and we may decide we want to hide this delegation. The *Refactoring* catalog tells us to take the following steps:

1. Create a simple delegating method on the server
2. For each client of the delegate:
   (a) Adjust the client to call the server's new method
   (b) Test
3. If no client needs to access the delegate any longer:
   (a) Remove the server's accessor for the delegate
   (b) Test

Refactoring is a step-by-step process. The steps are smaller than you might initially expect. Most refactorings tend to take from a minute to an hour to apply; the average is a few minutes. So, if a refactoring takes a few minutes, the steps are even smaller.

The steps themselves are generally *not* refactorings, because many of them leave the code in a broken or indeterminate state. Refactorings are *behavior-preserving* transformations, whereas the steps in any specific refactoring may temporarily break the code.

Step 1: Create a delegating method

We jump right in and create the method we need:

```
class Rectangle
  def left_edge
    @top_left.x
  end
end
```

Note that the clients of this class are unchanged: No code is calling this new method yet. (If we were feeling particularly nervous, or if an interruption seemed imminent, we could run our tests and check in the code at this point.)

Step 2: Adjust every client

One way to find the clients is to temporarily make the delegate private and run your tests. (If you do this, put it back to public visibility before changing the clients so you don't break any clients.)

This is where a good suite of tests can prove invaluable, especially in a large code-base. In a statically typed language such as Java or C# the compiler can tell you when there's a client using the now-private accessor. But in Ruby we are forced to rely on run-time checks—and the best kind are self-checking automated tests—or on reading the code. Refactoring tested code is significantly safer and faster than refactoring untested code, because the tests help us avoid slips.

The test run shows us that the following client code needs to be changed:

```ruby
class TranslationTest < Test::Unit::TestCase
  def test_translate_should_move_left_edge
    rect = Rectangle.new(Point.new(6.3, 5.0), 2.0, 2.0)
    rect.translate(-3.5, 1.0)
    assert_equal(2.8, rect.top_left.x)
  end
end
```

We replace the **Message Chain** with a call to the new delegating method:

```ruby
def test_translate_should_move_left_edge
  rect = Rectangle.new(Point.new(6.3, 5.0), 2.0, 2.0)
  rect.translate(-3.5, 1.0)
  assert_equal(2.8, rect.left_edge)
end
```

Step 3: Test after adjusting each call

Even though refactorings have the goal of creating an improved system at the end of the refactoring, many of them also have *safe points* along the way (think of *bases* in baseball or the children's game of tag; they may not be the ultimate destination, but at least you can't get tagged while you're on the base).

So, although we've made only one very simple change, we can stop, run the tests, and make sure we're okay so far. At this moment we may have some "old-style" clients and some "new-style" clients; our design embodies two different approaches in the midst of refactoring, and the system is not as clean as it will be in the end. Nevertheless, we have a green bar, we're safe on a *base,* and so we could check in right now if necessary, ready to pick up again tomorrow perhaps.

Imagine holding your breath while the system is in an unsafe state and then letting it go when the tests run correctly. This mild tension and release feels so much better than the feeling you get where you're halfway through one thing and you realize you want to do something else before you finish, and so on, and so on, until you're juggling five balls instead of one.

Large refactorings use this idea of bases as well. It's even more important in large refactorings. If it will take months to clean out the remnants of some decision, we *must* have safe points along the way.

Step 4: Remove the server's accessor

After we have changed all the relevant clients, we may discover that the accessor is no longer used. We can shrink the server's API by removing it:

```
class Rectangle
  attr_reader :top_left, :width, :height

  def left_edge
   @top_left.x
  end
end
```

becomes

```
class Rectangle
  attr_reader :width, :height

  def left_edge
   @top_left.x
  end
end
```

Step 5: Test again

We've reached another base, so we run the tests again and commit the code. At this point we've finished applying *Hide Delegate.*

The Generic Refactoring Micro-Process

A book on refactoring may list 20 or 50 refactorings, however those are just a sample of the common ones. You often create your own refactorings for a specific situation.

Many refactorings share the same abstract shape, which we can document as a micro-process:

1. Check whether the refactoring will run into any problems
2. Introduce a new code element
3. For each thing to migrate:
   (a) Migrate one client of the old element to use the new one
   (b) Test
4. Delete the old element
5. Test

This is a safe approach. The unsafe alternative is to change the old mechanism to use the new one, migrate everything in one bound, and hope for the best.

Large refactorings—those composed of smaller refactorings—use this approach as well. Indeed, it's fundamental to large refactorings that they keep the system working during a migration, as it could take hours, days, or even weeks.

There are a variety of ways for each of those steps (Check, Introduce, For each, Migrate, Delete, Test) to be realized; we've noted some of the possibilities in the following sections. These can be assembled to build up many new refactorings.

Check

These actions confirm that something is true.

- *Prove:* Prove (formally or informally) that the proposed refactoring is safe.
- *Look:* Look in the code to see if there is anything that would interfere with the refactoring to come. For example, you can't rename `f()` to `g()` if `g()` already exists.
- *Assert:* Introduce an assertion, code that verifies that some condition is true as you expect at a particular point. Use assertions in conjunction with tests, but recognize that they can only verify the cases the tests cover.

Introduce

These actions introduce a new element of some sort.

- *Add a new field, method, or class:* It will initially be unused, but it can be a target for new usages. For example, you might create a new empty method that will soon get code moved over from an existing method.

- *Introduce a new mechanism delegating to the old:* You can migrate things to use the new method, then inline the old method into the new.

- *Introduce a new, independent mechanism:* Migrate from the old mechanism to the new one.

- *Copy:* Copy code. For example, when you *Extract Method,* you copy the original code to the newly created method. We are not advocating copy-and-paste programming; two copies of the code will temporarily exist, but one will have been deleted by the time we reach the end of this refactoring micro-process.

For each

This action lets you look at all occurrences of something.

- *Iterate* over all uses of the code you want to change. Depending on the type of refactoring, this could involve calls, conditional branches, records, tables, methods, fields, classes, references, and so on.

Migrate

These actions take you from an old way of doing something to the new way.

- *Move a user of the old mechanism to the new one:* For example, change a reference from the old to the new.

- *Replace:* Replace something by its equivalent.

- *Adjust to a new context:* For example, the code used in *Extract Method* may need declarations, parameters, etc. to be modified.

- *Rename:* Giving a code element a more meaningful or intention-revealing name.

- *Swap two independent things:* For example, two statements that have no possible effect on each other can be swapped. This can be used to harmonize code fragments that would have the same text if it weren't for slight differences in the order of statements.

- *Propagate a constant:* When a "variable" has a constant value, replace the variable with the constant.

Delete

These actions eliminate elements.

- *Delete dead code:* Get rid of code that can never be executed.
- *Delete code with no effects:* For example, eliminate an empty method or class.
- *Deprecate:* For code that can't be deleted (because external uses must be accommodated), mark it to discourage new uses.

Test

The Generic Refactoring micro-process has a test run after each turn through the loop, and once again at the end. In practice, especially if you have comprehensive tests, you can take some shortcuts. For example, if you're moving a method you might have 25 references to it in the old place. You could move the first reference, test, move the second reference, test, and then move ten more before testing again once you're sure you have the pattern. Whether you take this shortcut will depend on a combination of factors: how long your tests take to run, how easily you can undo if you make a mistake, or how hard it is for you to check in files.

When the tests pass, it's usually worth checking in your code. Even if you are only halfway through the steps in one refactoring, creating safe bases as you go can significantly relieve the pressure to complete the task in one sitting.

It's important to stress again: Refactoring is only safe in the presence of good tests. Firstly because there's no compiler or static type checks to tell you when some subtle, but unwanted, typing error (pun intended) has occurred. And secondly because refactoring tools for Ruby are in their infancy, and even automated refactoring tools aren't perfect.

Exercises

Exercise 3.1: Small Steps

Pick any refactoring from Fields' *Refactoring, Ruby Edition* [11] and identify a place where the approach builds in small steps even though larger steps could work.

See page 216 for solution ideas.

Exercise 3.2: Inverse Refactorings

When we refactor, we're trying to respond to the forces affecting code. Sometimes what was a good change today no longer looks good tomorrow, and we find ourselves reversing a refactoring.

Following is a list of refactorings. Next to each refactoring, write the name of the refactoring that undoes its effects.

A. Collapse Hierarchy

B. Extract Method

C. Hide Delegate

D. Inline Temp

E. Parameterize Method

F. Rename Method

See page 216 for solution ideas.

What's Next

We've discussed the overall process of refactoring and the environment needed to tackle refactoring safely and productively; we've examined in detail the steps that make up a single refactoring move; and we've explored a generic pattern for refactoring. Before we move into the main body of the book we'll say a few words about what you can do to develop your refactoring skills in the longer term.

<small>CHAPTER 4</small>

Refactoring Practice

One of the premises of this book is that refactoring is a skill and benefits from practice. Look for opportunities to practice and use this skill.

Read Other Books

All the books in the bibliography will repay their study. But if you haven't yet acquired Fields et al.'s *Refactoring, Ruby Edition* [11], you should seriously consider doing so: The exercises in this book touch on perhaps half of the refactorings cataloged in the Fields book. Tools are getting better at the mechanics of refactoring support, but it will be a long time before they effectively cover every aspect of refactoring in the catalog.

Practice Refactoring

Find ways to make refactoring part of your daily life.

- *Build refactoring into your routine.* Knowing how to refactor isn't worth much unless it's applied. Resolve to make your code "lean and clean." On an XP team, this is part of everyday life. But even heavily design-driven approaches expect programmers to implement the design well.

- *Build testing into your routine.* There's an old adage (as so many are), "If it ain't broke, don't fix it." (How many times has the last "simple change" caused an unexpected bug?) In programming, the downside of applying this adage is that the code just gets uglier and uglier.

Refactoring is able to go against this rule because of two mechanisms: refactorings that are systematic and safe, and a supply of tests to verify that the transformations have been done correctly. Don't neglect your tests.

- *Take small steps.* Often, noticing a smell is relatively easy, compared with working out how to get "there" from "here." Practice breaking up the larger refactorings (such as *Tease Apart Inheritance*) into small, safe steps. Prefer transformations in which the system moves from good state to good state. When you refactor, prefer a *small steps but safer* approach over a *fast but not always safe* approach. Keep the refactoring cycle in mind.

- *Get help from others.* Get other peoples' opinions about your code, whether through pair programming, design and code reviews, or simply bugging your neighbor. Something we had hammered home to us while writing this book is that almost any code can be improved (and sometimes we get to take advantage of a whole Internet's worth of help!).

- *Add to the refactoring catalog.* As you work on your own code, look out for transformations that aren't documented anywhere; share and discuss them with your colleagues.

Exercises to Try

Here are some practice exercises you can try regularly, either alone or as a team *dojo*.

- *Scavenger Hunt/Smell of the Week:* Pick a smell, and find and eliminate as many occurrences of it as you can. Every week, search for a new smell.

- *Re-Refactor:* Pick a good-sized piece of code (either your own, or one of the larger examples in the back of this book would work). Each day, start from the initial version, and refactor as far as you can in ten minutes. Do you sense the same things each day? Do you get farther?

- *Just Refactor:* Pick or develop a project. Spend ten minutes refactoring. (Each day, start where you left off the day before.)

- *Inhale/Exhale:* Find code demonstrating some smell. Apply a refactoring that addresses it. Then apply the refactoring that reverses that one. Repeat this twice more. This will give you a sense of what it's like to put in a problem, as well as take it out.

- *Defactoring/Malfactoring:* "Defactoring" and "malfactoring" are names we use for malicious refactoring: *worsening* the design of existing code. Take some code, and "refactor" it to make it as smelly as possible. (It's harder than it sounds.) In addition to providing practice at refactoring, this may also help you realize when you're unintentionally malfactoring during development. Be sure to restore the original after you've had your fun.

- *Follow Your Nose:* Pick a code smell in a good-sized project. Eliminate it, and then review the changed code looking for other smells (this book's *What to Look for Next* sections will help). For each of the smells you now see, repeat. And so on. After 30 or 45 minutes, review both the resulting code and the journey you traveled. Is there more to do? Did all of the moves pay off? Did you go around in circles at any point?

- *Harmonizing:* Many of the code smells described in this book are fundamentally about some kind of duplication: identical code, similar code, code with similar structure, code with similar effects. Duplication isn't always obvious, and sometimes the code needs to be changed to reveal it. You can often make refactoring moves that will make latent duplication become explicit. Practice harmonizing things that want to be similar.

    For example, you may see code with the same effect, but using a different algorithm; you can substitute one of the algorithms so you can move to a single copy. Or suppose you have essentially the same method in two subclasses, except they have different names. You can rename them to the same name, so that you could pull the method into the parent. Or perhaps you have two methods that have some parts that are similar and other parts that are unique; you can tease apart the method so the similar parts are identical and the unique parts are separate, and then eliminate the duplication.

- *Refactoring Kata:* A kata is a martial arts exercise that you repeat every day, for practice and to help get into the rhythm of the art. (A traditional series might be a defense against four opponents.) Develop a kata for refactoring: a program where you'll apply a fixed series of refactorings. Pick a series of smells and refactorings that you see or use often—for example, it might include some open secrets, some long methods, some observed data to duplicate, and some responsibilities to rebalance. This will give you a chance to hone your editing skills and your understanding of your environment, as well as practice "smelling" and refactoring.

Participate in the Community

All of the preceding exercises work great on your own code, or on the larger exercises we've provided toward the back of this book. Or you could pick an open source project and practice on that; after you're done, you may have an improvement you can submit back to the community!

We're interested in your experience with these exercises, and with refactoring in general, so please feel free to write. The best place to do that is via this book's mailing list at `http://groups.google.com/group/refactoring-workbook`.

Exercise

Exercise 4.1: Get to Know the Refactorings

There is not a one-to-one relationship between refactorings and smells; as you work through the exercises in this book you'll run into the same refactorings again and again. For example, *Extract Method* is a tool that can fix many problems.

A. For each of the refactorings covered in Fields et al.'s *Refactoring, Ruby Edition* [11], list each smell it can help to fix. (Hint: Use the *What to Do* sections for each smell catalogued in Part II, "Code Smells," later in this book.)

B. Which refactorings fix the most smells?

C. Which refactorings aren't mentioned by any of the smells? Why not?

D. Does this list suggest any other smells we haven't covered?

See page 216 for solution ideas.

What's Next

That concludes our brief overview of the art of refactoring. It's now time to address the specifics. As we mentioned in Chapter 2, "The Refactoring Cycle," perhaps the most difficult part of the refactoring cycle is in recognizing code that needs to be refactored. Part II, "Code Smells," looks in detail at all of the common—and some of the not so common—code smells; by doing the exercises you'll learn how to recognize and eliminate them. Then Part III, "Programs to Refactor," provides you with a few complete applications, each of which is full of the kind of problems you'll encounter during real-life development.

PART II
Code Smells

## CHAPTER 5

Measurable Smells

The smells in this chapter are similar. They're dead easy to detect. They're objective (after you decide on a way to count and a maximum acceptable score). They're odious.

And, they're common.

You can think of these smells as being caught by a software metric. Each metric tends to catch different aspects of why code isn't as good as it could be. Some metrics measure variants of code length; others try to measure the connections between methods or objects; others measure a distance from an ideal.

Most metrics seem to correlate with length, so we tend to worry about size first (usually noticeable as a **Large Module** or **Long Method**). But if a metric is easy to compute, we'll use it as an indicator that some section of code deserves a closer look.

Metrics are indicators, not absolutes. It's very easy to get into the trap of *making numbers* without addressing the total complexity. So don't refactor just for a better number; make sure it really improves your code.

The smells in this chapter are the easiest to identify. They're not necessarily the easiest to fix.

There are other metrics that have been applied to software. Many of them are simply refinements of code length. Pay attention when things feel like they're getting too big.

In this chapter we'll cover the following smells:

- **Comments**, in which the code includes text to explain what's happening

- **Long Method**, in which a method is too long to be manageable

- **Large Module**, in which a class or module is too large to represent a meaningful abstraction

- **Long Parameter List**, in which a method needs too much information in order to get its job done

Comments

What to Look For

- The code contains a comment. (Some IDEs make these more obvious by color-coding comments.)

Why This Is a Problem

↝ **Flexibility:** Any comment that explains the code must be kept in step if the code is changed.

⋈ **Duplication:** Most comments can be reflected just as well in the code itself. For example, the goal of a method can often be communicated as well through its name as it can through a comment.

◁ **Communication:** Comments that say something slightly different than the code create cognitive drag—or even mistrust—and slow the reader down.

When to Leave It

Don't delete comments that are pulling their own weight—such as rdoc API documentation. Some comments can be particularly helpful—those that tell why something is done a particular way (or why it wasn't), or those that cite algorithms that are not obvious (where a simpler algorithm won't do).

How It Got This Way

Comments may be present for the best of reasons: The author realizes that something isn't as clear as it could be and adds a comment.

What to Do

- When a comment explains a code fragment, you can often use *Extract Method* to pull the fragment out into a separate method. The comment will often suggest a name for the new method.

- When a comment explains what a method does (better than the method's name!), use *Rename Method* using the comment as the basis of the new name.

- When a comment explains preconditions, consider using *Introduce Assertion* to replace the comment with code.

What to Look for Next

⋈ **Duplication:** Often the code fragments broken out of along method will do similar things in similar ways; it may be possible to identify some duplication among them.

◎ **Abstraction:** Creating names for code blocks helps to relate the design to the application's domain. Review the names in the area you changed for consistency.

Long Method
What to Look For

- A method has a large number of lines. (We're immediately suspicious of any method with more than five lines.)

Why This Is a Problem

⤳ **Flexibility:** A **Long Method** is guaranteed to be a **Greedy Method**—at least two responsibilities are coupled together in one place, which in turn leads to **Divergent Change.**

♭ **Testability:** It can be difficult to isolate individual behaviors of a **Long Method** for testing; and if a method does too much it may also be difficult to create fixtures that contain enough context for the method to work properly.

When to Leave It

It may be that a somewhat longer method is just the best way to express something. (Like almost all smells, the length is a warning sign, not a guarantee of a problem.)

How It Got This Way

You can think of it as the Columbo syndrome. Columbo was the TV detective who always had "just one more thing." A method starts down a path and, rather than break the flow or identify the helper classes, the author adds one more thing. Code is often easier to write than it is to read, so there's a temptation to write fragments that are too big.

What to Do

- Use *Extract Method* to break up the method into smaller pieces. Look for comments or white space delineating interesting fragments. You want to extract methods that are semantically meaningful, not just introduce a function call every seven lines.
- You may find other refactorings (those that clean up straight-line code, conditionals, and variable usage) helpful before you even begin splitting up the method.
- If the method doesn't separate easily into pieces, consider *Replace Method with Method Object* to turn the method into a separate object.

It's natural to worry about the performance hit from increasing the number of method calls, but most of the time this is a non-issue. By getting the code as clean as possible before worrying about performance, you have the opportunity to gain big insights that can restructure systems and algorithms in a way that dramatically increases performance.

What to Look for Next

⋈ **Duplication:** Often the code fragments broken out of a **Long Method** do similar things in similar ways; it may be possible to identify some duplication among them.

◁ **Communication:** Creating names for code fragments helps to relate the design to the application's domain. Review the names in the area you changed for consistency.

◎ **Abstraction:** The signatures of the new methods may suggest a missing class, or new structure may be revealed in the original method.

⤳ **Flexibility:** Review the new methods for **Feature Envy**; with more small pieces you now have the opportunity to move code to more "natural" homes.

Large Module

What to Look For

- A class or module has a large number of instance variables, methods, or just lines of code.

Why This Is a Problem

↯ **Testability:** A **Large Module** is usually difficult to test, either because it depends on many other modules or because it is difficult or time-consuming to create instances in isolation.

⤳ **Flexibility:** The module represents too many responsibilities folded together— that is, every **Large Module** is also a **Greedy Module**.

How It Got This Way

Large modules get big a little bit at a time. The developer keeps adding just one more capability to a module until eventually it grows too big. Sometimes the problem is a lack of insight into the parts that make up the whole module.

What to Do

In general, you're trying to break up the module. This usually proceeds piecemeal:

- Very often a review of the module reveals a composite of other smells, such as **Long Methods**, **Data Clumps**, and **Temporary Fields**; fix these smells first.

- To break up the module further, use *Extract Class* or *Extract Module* if you can identify a new piece that has part of this module's responsibilities.

- If you have a large class, you might try *Extract Subclass* if you can divide responsibilities between the class and a new subclass.

- Sometimes a class is big because it's a GUI class, and it represents both a display component and a model. In this case, you can use *Duplicate Observed Data* to help extract a domain class.

What to Look for Next

⋈ **Duplication:** As you peel off each piece of the **Large Module** you may discover it has similar responsibilities or interface to an existing module.

◁ **Communication:** Dividing up confused responsibilities, and giving names to them, helps the reader relate the code to the real domain. Review the names (see Chapter 6) used in the slimmer module and everything you extracted.

Long Parameter List

What to Look For

- A method has more than one or two parameters.

- A method yields more than one or two objects to an associated block.

Why This Is a Problem

• **Simplicity:** A **Long Parameter List** often indicates that a method has more than one responsibility. Sometimes the parameters have no meaningful grouping—they don't go together. In such cases it may be that the method, or the objects it uses, doesn't represent a meaningful and cohesive abstraction in the problem domain.

⤳ **Flexibility:** A **Long Parameter List** represents a large number of pieces of shared information between the caller and called code. If either changes, the parameter list is likely to need changing too.

◁ **Communication:** A lot of parameters represent a lot to remember—the programmer has to remember not only what objects to pass, but in which order. More succinct APIs are easier and quicker to use.

When to Leave It

This is one of those places where a smell doesn't always equate to a problem. You might smell a **Long Parameter List** but decide it's right for the situation at hand—for example, to avoid the called method picking up a dependency that you don't want it to have. Ensure that your changes don't upset this balance.

How It Got This Way

You might be trying to minimize coupling between objects. Instead of the called object being aware of relationships between classes, you let the caller locate everything; then the method concentrates on what it is being asked to do with the pieces.

The method may have acquired many parameters because the programmer generalized it to deal with multiple variations by creating a general algorithm with a lot of control parameters.

What to Do

- If a parameter's value can be obtained from another object this one already knows, use *Replace Parameter with Method.*

- If the parameters come from a single object, try *Preserve Whole Object*.
- If the data is not from one logical object, you still might group them via *Introduce Parameter Object*.

What to Look for Next

▷◁ **Duplication:** Sometimes a method's clients all have to jump through the same hoops in order to call it. Check for **Duplicated Code** among the callers.

◁ **Communication:** Parameters add to the cognitive load required to understand a class's interface; all of the above refactorings help to hide detail. Review all of this class's method signatures looking for **Data Clumps** and naming patterns.

▽ **Size:** The amount of code required to call a method can be large when the method requires a lot of unrelated parameters. Look for signs of **Feature Envy** and **Open Secret** around the objects you are now passing as parameters to the method.

Exercises

Exercise 5.1: Comments

Consider this code:

```
class Matcher
  def match(expected, actual, clip_limit, delta)
    # Clip "too-large" values
    actual = actual.map { |val| [val, clip_limit].min }

    # Check for length differences
    return false if actual.length != expected.length

    # Check that each entry is within expected +/- delta
    actual.each_index { |i|
      return false if (expected[i] - actual[i]).abs > delta
    }
    return true
  end
end
```

A. Use *Extract Method* to make the comments in `match()` redundant.

B. Can everything important about the code be communicated using the code alone? Or do comments have a place?

C. Find some code you wrote recently. Odds are good that you commented it. Can you eliminate the need for some of those comments by making the code reflect your intentions more directly?

See page 217 for solution ideas.

Exercise 5.2: Long Method

Consider this code:

```ruby
class Robot
  attr_reader :location, :bin

  def move_to(location)
    @location = location
  end

  def pick
    @bin = @location.take
  end

  def release
    @location.put(@bin)
    @bin = nil
  end
end

class Machine
  attr_reader :name, :bin

  def initialize(name, location)
    @name = name
    @location = location
  end

  def take
    result = @bin
    @bin = nil
    return result
  end

  def put(bin)
    @bin = bin
  end
end
```

```
class Report
  def Report.report(out, machines, robot)
    out.print "FACTORY REPORT\n"
    machines.each do |machine|
      out.print "Machine #{machine.name}"
      out.print "bin=#{machine.bin}" if machine.bin != nil
      out.print "\n"
    end
    out.print "\n"
    out.print "Robot"
    if robot.location != nil
      out.print "location=#{robot.location.name}"
    end
    out.print "bin=#{robot.bin}" if robot.bin != nil
    out.print "\n"
    out.print "========\n"
  end
end
```

(In the code download you can find Rspec examples showing how these classes interact.)

A. In `Report.report`, circle four blocks of code to show which functions you might extract in the process of refactoring this code.

B. Rewrite the `report` method as four statements, as if you had done *Extract Method* for each block.

C. Does it make sense to extract a one-line method?

See page 217 for solution ideas.

Exercise 5.3: Large Class

Consider the API for the String class in Ruby 1.8.6:

```
str % arg
str * integer
str + integer
str << fixnum
str << obj
str.concat(fixnum)
str.concat(obj)
```

```
str <=> other_str
str == obj
str =~ obj
str[fixnum]
str[fixnum, fixnum]
str[range]
str[regexp]
str[regexp, fixnum]
str[other_str]
str[fixnum] = fixnum
str[fixnum] = new_str
str[fixnum, fixnum] = new_str
str[range] = aString
str[regexp] = new_str
str[regexp, fixnum] = new_str
str[other_str] = new_str
str.capitalize
str.capitalize!
str.casecmp(other_str)
str.center(integer, padstr)
str.chomp(separator=$/)
str.chomp!(separator=$/)
str.chop
str.chop!
str.concat(fixnum)
str.concat(obj)
str.count([other_str]+)
str.crypt(other_str)
str.delete([other_str]+)
str.delete!([other_str]+>)
str.downcase
str.downcase!
str.dump
str.each(separator=$/) {|substr| block }
str.each_byte {|fixnum| block }
str.each_line(separator=$/) {|substr| block }
str.empty?
str.eql?(other)
str.gsub(pattern, replacement)
str.gsub(pattern) {|match| block }
str.gsub!(pattern, replacement)
str.gsub!(pattern) {|match| block }
str.hash
str.hex
str.include? other_str
str.include? fixnum
```

```
str.index(substring [, offset])
str.index(fixnum [, offset])
str.index(regexp [, offset])
str.insert(index, other_str)
str.inspect
str.intern
str.length
str.ljust(integer, padstr=' ')
str.lstrip
str.lstrip!
str.match(pattern)
str.next
str.next!
str.oct
str.replace(other_str)
str.reverse
str.reverse!
str.rindex(substring [, fixnum])
str.rindex(fixnum [, fixnum])
str.rindex(regexp [, fixnum])
str.rjust(integer, padstr=' ')
str.rstrip
str.rstrip!
str.scan(pattern)
str.scan(pattern) {|match, ...| block }
str.slice(fixnum)
str.slice(fixnum, fixnum)
str.slice(range)
str.slice(regexp)
str.slice(regexp, fixnum)
str.slice(other_str)
str.slice(fixnum)
str.slice(fixnum, fixnum)
str.slice(range)
str.slice(regexp)
str.slice(regexp, fixnum)
str.slice(other_str)
str.slice!(fixnum)
str.slice!(fixnum, fixnum)
str.slice!(range)
str.slice!(regexp)
str.slice!(other_str)
str.split(pattern=$;, [limit])
str.squeeze([other_str]*)
str.squeeze!([other_str]*)
str.strip
```

```
str.strip!
str.sub(pattern, replacement)
str.sub(pattern) {|match| block }
str.sub!(pattern, replacement)
str.sub!(pattern) {|match| block }
str.succ
str.succ!
str.sum(n=16)
str.swapcase
str.swapcase!
str.to_f
str.to_i(base=10)
str.to_s
str.to_str
str.to_sym
str.tr(from_str, to_str)
str.tr!(from_str, to_str)
str.tr_s(from_str, to_str)
str.tr_s!(from_str, to_str)
str.unpack(format)
str.upcase
str.upcase!
str.upto(other_str) {|s| block }
```

A. Why does this class have so many methods?

B. Go through the methods listed and categorize them into five to ten major areas of responsibility.

C. Many of the methods have aliases (e.g., next and succ, [] and slice). What are the tradeoffs in having aliases?

D. Most String methods have two versions—for example, str.reverse and str.reverse!. (The first form returns a new string; the ! form changes the existing string in place.) What are the consequences of having the two types of methods?

E. On balance, do you consider the size of class String to be a smell?

F. In Java, class Object has 11 methods, whereas in Ruby and Smalltalk it has many times this number. Why the difference? Talk to a Java person and consider whether you think Ruby's version smells.

See page 218 for solution ideas.

Exercise 5.4: Smells and Refactorings

Consider these smells:

A. Comments
B. Large Module
C. Long Method
D. Long Parameter List

For each refactoring in the following list, write the letter for the smell(s) it might help cure:

___ Duplicate Observed Data

___ Extract Class

___ Extract Method

___ Extract Subclass

___ Introduce Assertion

___ Introduce Parameter Object

___ Preserve Whole Object

___ Rename Method

___ Replace Parameter with Method

See page 220 for solution ideas.

Exercise 5.5: Triggers

Consider the smells described in this chapter.

A. Which of these do you find most often? Which do you create most often?

B. To stop children from sucking their thumbs, some parents put a bad-tasting or spicy solution on the child's thumb. This serves as a trigger that reminds the child not to do that. What triggers can you give yourself to help you recognize when you're just beginning to create one of these smells?

See page 220 for solution ideas.

CHAPTER 6

Names

The creation of a good mental model is one of the key challenges in developing software. There are several tools people use to help with this:

- Project dictionaries
- Domain vocabularies, ontologies, and languages
- XP-style metaphors

How we name things is important. Good names perform several functions:

- They provide a vocabulary for discussing our domain.
- They communicate intent.
- They support subtle expectations about how the system works.
- They support each other in a system of names.

It's hard to pick good names, but it's worth the effort. Ward Cunningham describes using a thesaurus to get just the right sense.

Some teams have coding standards and naming standards that affect how names are chosen. You may find these guidelines helpful:

- Use verbs for manipulators, and nouns and/or adjectives for accessors.
- Use terms consistently: Have each word mean the same wherever it is used; give each concept the same name wherever it occurs; and use different words for different things.
- Prefer one-word names.
- Value communication most.

Don't worry too much about getting each name right the first time, but do ensure you change a name immediately when a better alternative suggests itself. Especially with tool support, it's not that hard to change a name; it's always worth investing a little energy in improving names as you modify code.

In this chapter we'll cover the following smells:

- **Type Embedded in Name**, in which names are coupled to types
- **Uncommunicative Name**, in which a name doesn't reveal the developer's intentions
- **Inconsistent Names**, in which domain vocabulary isn't standardized

Type Embedded in Name
What to Look For

- Names that are compound words, consisting of a word plus the type of the argument(s)—for example, a method `add_course(course)`.

- Hungarian notation, where the type of an object is encoded into the name—for example, `i_count` as an integer variable.

- Variable names that reflect their type rather than their purpose or role.

Why This Is a Problem

⤳ **Flexibility:** The name of a reference has been coupled to the type of the object it references; if either changes we could introduce some cognitive drag.

◎ **Abstraction:** Different names for the same thing can hide abstractions.

When to Leave It

This smell is weakest when applied to method names: Sometimes you need to distinguish methods from each other according to the types of their parameters or return values. (An example from core Ruby is the "conversion" methods: `to_s`, `to_a`, `to_i`, `to_f`, etc.)

How It Got This Way

The type may originally have been added to help with communication: Hungarian notation is often introduced as part of a coding standard—for example, in a pointer-based language such as C it is useful to know that `**ppc` is in fact a character. Some programmers or teams use a convention where a prefix indicates that something is a member variable (`_count` or `m_count`). In Ruby, this is redundant—we already use `@` to indicate member variables.

What to Do

- Use *Rename Method* (or field or constant or parameter) to a name that communicates intent without being so tied to a type.

What to Look for Next

⋈ **Duplication:** Removing the type names may reveal other duplication. Look for **Alternative Modules with Different Interfaces**.

Uncommunicative Name
What to Look For
A name doesn't communicate its intent well enough. Examples of this can include:

- One- or two-character names
- Names with vowels omitted
- Numbered variables (e.g., `pane1`, `pane2`, and so on)
- Odd abbreviations
- Misleading names

Why This Is a Problem
◁ **Communication:** Poor names deceive the reader; they make it harder to build a mental picture of what's going on, and they can be misinterpreted. They also hurt the flow of reading as the reader must slow down to interpret the names.

↝ **Flexibility:** Very short names can be difficult to change, even with automated refactoring tools.

When to Leave It
Some teams use short names such as `i`, `j`, or `k` for loop indexes or `c` for characters; these aren't too confusing if the scope is limited. Similarly, you may occasionally find that numbered variables communicate better.

How It Got This Way
When you first implement something, you have to name things somehow. You give the best name you can think of at the time and move on. Later, you may have an insight that lets you pick a better name.

What to Do
- Use *Rename Method* (or field, constant, etc.) to give it a better name.

What to Look for Next
⋈ **Duplication:** Look for places where the same name means different things, or the same thing has different names.

Inconsistent Names
What to Look For

- One name is used in one place, and a different name is used for the same thing somewhere else. For example, in a single application you might see `add`, `store`, `put`, and `place` for the same basic method.

Why This Is a Problem

◁ **Communication:** Multiple names (for no reason) make it hard for the reader.

⋈ **Duplication:** The different names may hide similar methods.

How It Got This Way

Different people may create the classes at different times. (People may forget to explore the existing classes before adding more.) Occasionally, you'll find people doing this intentionally (but misguidedly) so they can distinguish the names.

What to Do

Pick the best name, and use *Rename Method* (or field, constant, etc.) to give the same name to the same things.

The Eiffel language uses a common pool of words for the names of its library features; the Rails framework also uses naming conventions extensively. You can use this technique as inspiration: Look to existing library names for the vocabulary you use.

What to Look for Next

⋈ **Duplication:** Addressing this smell can make classes become more similar than when they started. Look for a duplication smell and eliminate it.

Exercises

Exercise 6.1: Names

Classify these method names as **Type Embedded in Name, Uncommunicative Name**, or OK.

___ `add_item(item)`

___ `do_it`

___ `get_nodes_array`

___ `get_data`

___ `make_it`

___ `multiply_int_int(int1, int2)`

___ `process_item`

___ `sort`

___ `spin`

See page 220 for solution ideas.

Exercise 6.2: Critique the Names

Which name would you expect to use?

A. To empty a window (onscreen)
```
window.clear
window.wash
window.erase
window.delete_all
```

B. For a stack
```
stack.add
stack.insert
stack.push
stack.add_to_front
```

C. For an editor (to get rid of the selected text)

```
selection.cut
selection.delete
selection.clear
selection.erase
```

D. As part of a file comparison program

```
line1.compare(line2)
line1.eql?(line2)
line1.identical_to(line2)
line1.matches(line2)
```

See page 221 for solution ideas.

Exercise 6.3: Superclasses

In each of the following scenarios you have a group of classes, and you want to introduce a superclass for them. What do you call it?

A. Car, Boat, Train

B. LaserPrinter, InkjetPrinter, NetworkPrinter

See page 221 for solution ideas.

Exercise 6.4: Method Names

A. You have classes Schedule and Course, and a method named `schedule.add_course(course)`. Later, you introduce a class Syllabus—a collection of Courses that behaves just like a single Course. So now `schedule.add_course(thing)` can add a Syllabus too. Is that a problem?

B. During development, you have classes Graph, Point, and Edge (in the mathematical sense) and a method `graph.add(point)`. Now you want to be able to add edges to a graph too. What new method(s) might you introduce to accomplish that?

See page 221 for solution ideas.

## CHAPTER 7

Unnecessary Complexity

Code is sometimes more complicated than it would have to be purely to solve the problem at hand. There are three main causes for this problem:

- Code shows the traces of its history, the leftovers from old ways of doing things; the current complexity of the code owes more to the past—and to the journey travelled—than to the present.
- The design has been over-generalized. This is often done in anticipation of future requirements, or for premature performance tuning.
- The original developers were unfamiliar with Ruby—they didn't know that there was a language feature or a library method that does what they needed.

Remove these problems when you run into them. You'll often find that this can lead to further insight and simplification.

In this chapter we'll cover the following smells:

- **Dead Code**, in which some code is unused
- **Speculative Generality**, in which code exists "just in case"
- **Greedy Method**, in which a method has more than one responsibility
- **Procedural Code**, in which code proceeds step by step
- **Dynamic Code Creation**, in which `class_eval` and friends are used to create code at run-time

Dead Code

What to Look For

- A variable, parameter, code fragment, method, module, or class is not used any-where (perhaps other than in tests).

Why This Is a Problem

▽ **Size:** **Dead Code** adds to the application's size, and thus to the amount of code that must be understood by developers and maintainers.

◁ **Communication:** It isn't always obvious when code is dead, and so the reader may take it as having a bearing on the behavior of his software. Indeed, **Dead Code** that is also incorrect or invalid may lead the developer seriously astray.

⤳ **Flexibility:** All code has dependencies on other code; but **Dead Code** may create de-pendencies where otherwise there would be none. These unnecessary couplings may, in turn, slow the pace of change for the code in these areas.

When to Leave It

If your application is a framework, it may include elements or hooks purely to support clients' needs, but which aren't needed by the framework itself.

How It Got This Way

Requirements have changed, or a new design has been introduced, without adequate cleanup. Or sometimes complicated logic results in some combinations of conditions that can't actually happen; you'll see this when simplifying conditionals.

What to Do

- Delete the unused code and any associated tests.

- The code you just deleted may have been the only client of some other code, so that in turn is now dead. Continue checking and deleting until you find no more **Dead Code.**

What to Look for Next

▽ **Size:** There are fewer code elements to be loaded and interpreted, and there is less code to read and search. You may find you now have a **Lazy Class** or a **Data Class,** for example.

◁ **Communication:** Removing unnecessary code elements may free up names from the application's domain. These names can now be reused, and it may be possible to give better names to existing code elements.

• **Simplicity:** The removal of unused code paths can render algorithms easier to understand and will often clear the way for further refactoring to simplify code that previously was too complex. Look out for **Special Case** logic in methods that you have recently thinned out.

Speculative Generality
What to Look For

- The application's design includes "hooks" to permit future adaptation or customization, and these hooks are only used in one way—or not at all—right now.
- Code is more complicated than it has to be for the currently implemented requirements.
- A class has only one subclass, or a method has only one caller, or a module is only used in one place.
- The names used in part of the application are abstract or overly general.

Lazy Class and Special Case are often indicators that the application at large may be suffering from Speculative Generality.

Why This Is a Problem

◁ Communication: Speculative abstractions can make the code harder to understand.

↝ Flexibility: Hooks and special cases can get in the way when you want to change current behavior. So, they can slow down the pace of development and maintenance, even creating "no-go" areas within an application. Dealing with such code often feels like "walking on eggshells."

When to Leave It

An application framework may have elements present to support clients' needs that, strictly speaking, aren't needed by the framework itself. Or perhaps some elements are used by test methods and they're exposed as *probe points* to allow a test to have privileged information about the class. Be careful though—this may indicate that you're missing an abstraction that you could test independently.

How It Got This Way

The code may have been built with the expectation that it will become more useful, but then it never does. When people try to outguess the needs of the code, they often add things for generality or for completeness that end up never being used. Sometimes the code has been used before, but is no longer needed because of new or revised ways of doing things. (Speculative Generality may be Dead Code that was created on purpose.)

What to Do

- For an unnecessary module, use the appropriate *Inline* refactoring on each method, class, and constant in the module.

- For an unnecessary class: If parents or children of the class seem like the right place for its behavior, fold it into one of them via *Collapse Hierarchy*. Otherwise, fold its behavior into its caller via *Inline Class*.

- For an unnecessary method, use *Inline Method* or *Remove Method*.

- For an unnecessary instance variable, remove all references to it.

- For an unnecessary parameter, use *Remove Parameter*.

What to Look for Next

◁ **Communication:** The removal of unnecessary code elements may free up names from the application's domain; those names can now be reused, so it may now be possible to give better names to existing code elements.

⤳ **Flexibility:** If you inlined anything, look again at the receiving code: Have you created a **Long Method** or **Large Module**? Have you created a **Greedy Method** or a **Greedy Module**?

▽ **Size:** Review the places where you removed code or parameters; look out now for a **Lazy Class** or some **Dead Code**.

Greedy Method

What to Look For

- A method does more than one job.
- A method has "and" in its name.
- The body of a method includes code at several different levels of abstraction.

Why This Is a Problem

◁ **Communication:** A code fragment that has two responsibilities intertwined is harder to read, and harder to name.

⤳ **Flexibility:** If one of the method's responsibilities must change, or has a defect, you often have to work hard to sidestep the method's other responsibilities—it can therefore be a challenge to avoid breaking other code.

↯ **Testability:** A method that does two things will be harder to test than if the responsibilities were separated.

A method that does two jobs is often said to violate the *Single Responsibility Principle* (SRP); see Robert Martin's *Agile Software Development: Principles, Patterns, and Practices* [21] for a broader explanation of the SRP.

How It Got This Way

When new behavior must be added, the quickest thing to do is often to weave it into existing code.

What to Do

- Consider the approaches to dealing with a **Long Method**—they will often work here just as well. Use *Extract Method* to hide detail behind an intention-revealing name.
- If the method makes extensive use of another object, treat and fix the **Feature Envy**.
- Look at the method's parameters: Do they come from different "parts" of the application? Are some of them domain related, whereas others are technology related? Look for ways to extract methods whose parameter lists are more consistent.

What to Look for Next

◁ **Communication:** If you extracted one or more methods, check the whole system of names in their receiving class(es) to ensure it is still consistent.

⋈ **Duplication:** Review any extracted methods for **Feature Envy** to ensure they have been sent to the right class. Check also for **Duplicated Code** to ensure they really are different from the others in the receiving class(es).

♩ **Testability:** Now that you have smaller decoupled methods, check your tests and test fixtures. You may find that these can be simplified too.

Procedural Code

What to Look For

- An algorithm proceeds step by step, possibly using one or more temporary variables to hold intermediate values.
- Code iterates over the contents of an `Array` or `Hash`, instead of using an approach based on `each`.
- A code fragment uses a local variable to cache an intermediate result.

Why This Is a Problem

⋈ **Duplication:** Every collection in Ruby (and indeed any class that includes the `Enumerable` module) already provides methods that iterate over its elements, so iterating in your own code is almost always a kind of **Reinvented Wheel**.

↝ **Flexibility:** Any method that iterates over a collection *and* does something with the elements is arguably a **Greedy Method**.

• **Simplicity:** Local variables, especially when used to manage iteration, can add clutter and obscure a method's flow. They can also hamper refactorings such as *Extract Method.*

◁ **Communication:** In any language, using the language's own idioms helps communicate the code's intent to the widest possible audience. In order to be maximally communicative, your code should be written using the styles and idioms of your community. **Procedural Code** is not idiomatic in Ruby circles.

When to Leave It

Sometimes a code fragment uses a well-named local variable to help explain the steps in an algorithm or the reason the design is like it is.

How It Got This Way

During test-driven development, a procedural solution is often the quickest next step to get from a red to a green bar. Or, the original code was written by someone not used to Ruby's more functional and object-oriented style.

What to Do

- If you're iterating over a collection, *Replace Loop with Collection Closure Method*—for example, using `select`, `reject`, or `collect`.

- If you have a temporary variable on which a series of operations is performed, *Replace Temp with Chain.*

What to Look for Next

◁ **Communication:** If you used *Replace Loop with Collection Closure Method* you may have extracted one or more methods to perform parts of the job; make sure these methods are well named and live on the appropriate class.

⤳ **Flexibility:** If you've converted a loop to a chain of method calls, you may have decoupled portions of the loop from each other. Look out for **Feature Envy** if sections of the chain no longer depend on the state of the current object.

Dynamic Code Creation

What to Look For

- Code uses `eval`, `class_eval`, or `module_eval` to build new code dynamically.

Why This Is a Problem

Dynamic code evaluation is a very powerful mechanism, and with great power comes great responsibility.

◁ **Communication:** The names of an application's classes and methods form the vocabulary that makes the code human-readable. That code becomes harder to read and understand when the abstractions are fluid or created late.

↯ **Testability:** Testing, or test-driving, anything that changes dynamically is an order of magnitude harder than normal test-driven development.

⤳ **Flexibility:** Dynamic code evaluation is difficult to debug, and often runs more slowly than the alternatives.

When to Leave It

Sometimes dynamic code evaluation is the only or best way to solve a particular problem. For example, it may be impossible to determine which methods a class must have until run-time.

How It Got This Way

It can be difficult to find the right set of abstractions to define a problem, and so it makes sense to build them dynamically as the need arises.

   Other times you might want to use the expressive power of standard Ruby classes and methods, but you only find out at run-time which ones you'll need and what they need to look like.

What to Do

- If your code uses the String form of `eval`, try to replace it with one of the block forms, or with calls to `define_method`; this at least provides some syntax safety.
- If you're using `method_missing`, replace it using *Replace Dynamic Receptor with Dynamic Method Definition*—for example, convert it to use `class_eval`.

- If it is absolutely necessary to use `eval`, but parsing the string is becoming a performance bottleneck, use *Move Eval from Run-time to Parse-time*.

What to Look for Next

⋈ **Duplication:** Moving evaluation from run-time to parse-time could introduce **Duplicated Code**; decide whether this trade-off is worth the price.

◁ **Communication:** Look for opportunities to hide dynamic evaluation behind helpful method names, to make your intentions clear to the reader.

Exercises

Exercise 7.1: Dead Code (Challenging)

Find an application or project that has undergone changes in requirements or design. Odds are good that it now contains dead code.

A. Find some dead code by reading through and simulating suspect areas by hand. How confident are you that this code is indeed redundant?

B. If you don't have them already, write thorough tests for all clients of this suspect code. Are you now more confident that the code can be removed?

C. Find an appropriate code coverage tool—such as Rcov (`http://rubyforge.org/projects/rcov/`)—and use it to analyze your test run. How confident are you now that this suspect code is redundant?

D. What does the coverage tool tell you about libraries and gems loaded by your code? Is that a problem? If yours is a Rails application, did you make use of all of the scaffolding provided? Is that a problem?

E. Modify the suspect code so that it is obviously broken, perhaps by having it raise an exception. (If you have `heckle` available, run it on your test suite.) Do you get any surprises when you rerun the tests? If not, delete the dead code.

F. Which of the preceding approaches worked best in your application? Which gave the best return on the effort involved? Repeat the exercise by finding another chunk of dead code, this time focusing on the technique(s) that gave the most benefit.

Exercise 7.2: Today versus Tomorrow

There are arguments for and against Speculative Generality being a smell. We can caricature them as follows:

• Some agile development methods, notably Extreme Programming, argue that Speculative Generality is a smell, and that you aren't going to need it. That is, make your code meet today's requirements, and don't try to anticipate which way tomorrow's requirements will go. (Thus an agile team is more likely to evolve a framework from an application than to build a framework and use it to create an application.)

• Another approach is to design for flexibility or to design for generality. This means that you should fully flesh out your classes based on the expected requirements.

When refactoring code you will often need to decide which approach is better for the particular case you're currently dealing with.

A. What are the forces that make it better to design for only today's requirements today?

B. What are the forces that make it better to design for tomorrow's requirements today?

See page 222 for solution ideas.

Exercise 7.3: Extraction Trade-Offs

Imagine you've found a Long Method or a Large Module, and you deal with it by extracting new methods or classes.

A. These extracted pieces will often have only one client—the original code. Have you just introduced a case of Speculative Generality? If not, why not?

B. Now jump six months into the future: A newcomer to the team looks at this refactored code, perhaps in order to change its behavior for a new requirement. Will the newcomer see Speculative Generality here?

C. What might you do now to help make it clear that Speculative Generality is not present?

See page 222 for solution ideas.

Exercise 7.4: Formatting Names

Consider the following method:

```
def display_full_name(out, person)
  out.write(person.first)
  out.write(" ")
  if person.middle != nil
    out.write(person.middle)
    out.write(" ")
  end
  out.write(person.last)
end
```

A. What are the clues that this is a Greedy Method?

B. Devise and carry out a sequence of changes that will remove the smell.

See page 223 for solution ideas.

Exercise 7.5: Procedural Code

Consider the following method:

```
class Cart
  def total_price
    total = 0
    @items.each { |item| total += item.price }
    return total
  end
end
```

A. Use the `inject` method to rewrite this code without an explicit iterator.

B. Looking again at the original code, why might `total_price` be considered a **Greedy Method**?

C. Refactor the method a second time, beginning again from the preceding code. This time around, fix the greediness first, and then fix the **Procedural Code**.

D. Compare your two refactored versions of the code, looking particularly at communication and flexibility.

See page 223 for solution ideas.

CHAPTER 8

Duplication

Duplication has been recognized for more than 30 years as the bane of the programmer's lot. How does duplication cause problems?

- There is more code to maintain (a conceptual and physical burden).

- Parts that vary are buried inside the parts that stay the same (a perceptual problem—it's hard to see the important stuff).

- Code variations often hide deeper similarities—it will be hard to see the deeper solution hidden within all the similar code.

- There's a tendency to fix a defect in one place and leave identical defects elsewhere unfixed. When you see two variations of something, it's hard to know which variation is the right pattern or if there's a good reason for the differences.

David Parnas introduced the idea of *information hiding:* A good module has a secret. By ensuring that a module keeps its secret, we usually reduce duplication. (See "On the criteria to be used in decomposing systems into modules" [25].)

Duplication is a root problem. Many other smells are special-case examples of duplication. Duplication is not always obvious, but it's critical to address it. Strive to make your code express each idea "once and only once." Don't repeat yourself.

In this chapter we'll cover the following smells:

- **Derived Value,** in which a hard-coded value could have been computed instead

- **Repeated Value,** in which a hard-coded value is repeated

- **Duplicated Code,** in which code has been copied

- **Alternative Modules with Different Interfaces,** in which the same problem has been solved more than once

Derived Value

What to Look For

- The code contains a hard-coded value that could also be obtained by calculating it from other values or referencing an appropriate constant.

Why This Is a Problem

⋈ **Duplication:** When a value is computed two different ways, it's prone to the two mechanisms diverging.

◁ **Communication:** Showing the relationship between values helps to document the design more clearly.

When to Leave It

Some tests may benefit from having a derived value: It may make the test more readable, and it may demonstrate an independent computation of the value.

How It Got This Way

Someone needed a value, so they put it in the code. On its own, perhaps it's not so bad, but often there are other values derived from or dependent on it. For example, we'll have a string defined as "banana" and a length variable of 6. If you change the string, you need to change the length variable; however, this is not obvious, and so a defect gets in.

What to Do

- Use *Replace Value with Expression* for the derived value.

What to Look for Next

⋈ **Duplication:** Cleaning up this duplication may make it easier to see other duplication. You may see examples of **Feature Envy**.

◎ **Abstraction:** By making explicit the fact that two values depend on each other, you may identify the need to wrap those values and calculations in a class. You may see this in the form of an **Open Secret**.

Repeated Value

What to Look For

- A hard-coded value—such as a GUI scaling factor or a text string—occurs more than once in the code and has the same meaning each time.

Why This Is a Problem

⋈ **Duplication:** Defects can enter if the value is changed in one place but not the other.

◁ **Communication:** When a value appears multiple times, it's not clear whether this is intentional or coincidental.

When to Leave It

The same value might actually mean different things. For example, two different modules might use the empty string as a default value. This is a coincidence and not an example of duplication. Nevertheless, you might improve communication by creating constants to give domain-related names to these default values.

Tests are often more readable when they simply use the value they want, but again you may sometimes pull out a symbolic constant if it better communicates your intent.

How It Got This Way

A programmer needs a value and puts it in the code; the value then embodies a requirement or a design choice. Later, someone needs the same value, so he either copies the original or independently makes the same choice.

What to Do

- If the value is genuinely a simple constant, use *Replace Magic Number with Symbolic Constant* to give it a meaningful name.
- Very often, the value is a clue to the existence of the hard form of **Duplicated Code**. Use *Extract Method* or *Form Template Method* on the repeated algorithm. Leave the value itself inline in the resulting code, unless naming it helps to explain or document the algorithm.
- If the values are strings (e.g., the text of dialog boxes), you may want to put them in some sort of mapping facility or use an internationalization library such as `ri18n`.

What To Look for Next

⋈ **Duplication:** Removing this duplication may make it easier to see other duplication.

◎ **Abstraction:** Removing this duplication may reveal the need for a new class responsible for the value.

Duplicated Code

What to Look For

- The easy form: Two fragments of code look nearly identical.
- The hard form: Two fragments of code have nearly identical effects (at any conceptual level).

Why This Is a Problem

▽ **Size:** The code is bigger than it has to be, with more to understand.

⤳ **Flexibility:** A design concept expressed more than once interferes with future changes; the change may have to be done in multiple places.

◁ **Communication:** Near-repetition interferes with how easily code is understood. (The reader must decide whether two things are really expressing one concept, and whether any differences are significant.)

When to Leave It

Sometimes, what appears to be duplication is in fact coincidental. In such a case, folding the two places together would confuse the reader and create friction against future change.

Very rarely, you might decide that the duplication is necessary to help the code communicate better, and choose to leave it in place.

How It Got This Way

Some duplication occurs because programmers work independently in different parts of the system, and they don't realize that they are creating almost identical code. Sometimes people realize there's duplication, but they don't have the time or inclination to remove it. Other times, duplication will be hidden by other smells; after those smells are fixed, the duplication becomes more obvious.

Perhaps the most common case occurs when the programmers intentionally duplicate code. They find some code that is "almost" right, so they copy-and-paste it into the new spot with some slight alterations. This often happens on a red bar during test-driven development, when it is imperative to get to the green bar as quickly as possible.

What to Do

- If the duplication is within a method or in two different methods in the same class or module: Use *Extract Method* to pull the common part out into a separate method.

- If the duplication is within two sibling classes: Use *Extract Method* to create a single method, then *Pull Up Method* (and *Pull Up Instance Variable* if needed) to bring the common parts together. Then you may be able to use *Form Template Method* to create a common algorithm in the parent and unique steps in the children.

- If the duplication is in two modules or in two unrelated classes: Either extract the common part into a new class or module, or decide that the smell is **Feature Envy** so the common code really belongs in only one place.

- In any of these cases, you may find that the two places aren't literally identical but that they have the same effect. Then you may do a *Substitute Algorithm* so that only one copy is involved.

What to Look for Next

◎ **Abstraction:** Look for ways to push related responsibilities together. You may find new classes waiting to emerge.

Alternative Modules with Different Interfaces

What to Look For

- Two classes or modules seem to be doing the same thing but are using different method names.

Why This Is a Problem

↝ **Flexibility:** Maintaining two similar chunks of code can be time-consuming and costly.

◁ **Communication:** Having different names for the same concept makes code harder to understand.

◎ **Abstraction:** Different names interfere with your ability to pull out common code.

When to Leave It

Even with Ruby's open classes, it's not always expedient to change interfaces (e.g., if both are in different libraries that you'd rather not own). Each library may have its own vision for the same concept, but you may be left with no good way to unify them.

How It Got This Way

People create similar code to handle similar situations, but don't realize the other code exists.

What to Do

Harmonize the classes or modules so that you can eliminate one of them.

1. Use *Rename Method* to make method names similar.

2. Use *Move Method*, *Add Parameter*, and *Parameterize Method* to make protocols (method signatures and approach) similar.

3. If you have two classes that are similar but not identical, use *Extract Superclass* after you have them reasonably well harmonized. For similar modules, extract a shared module or class that they can both use.

4. Remove the extra class or module if possible.

What to Look for Next

⋈ **Duplication:** You may be able to extract common helper or superclasses.

Exercises

Exercise 8.1: Rakefile

Consider the following fragment of a Rakefile:

```
require 'rake/contrib/sshpublisher'

file '.published' => ['sparky.html', 'sparky.rb'] do
  Rake::SshFilePublisher.new('www.ruby-refactoring.com',
    '/var/www/tools', '.', 'sparky.html').upload
  Rake::SshFilePublisher.new('www.ruby-refactoring.com',
    '/usr/lib/cgi-bin', '.', 'sparky.rb').upload
  touch '.published'
end

desc "copy all files to the live deploy locations"
task :deploy => '.published'
```

A. Identify at least three sets of duplicated strings. Which kind of duplication does each represent?

B. Eliminate each type of duplication in turn.

C. Was some duplication harder to eliminate than others? Starting again from the original code, try removing the smells in a different order. Does that change your solution? Does it alter the relative difficulty of each refactoring?

D. This example has no tests; did you make any mistakes while refactoring? What could you haved one to make the process less error prone?

See page 225 for solution ideas.

Exercise 8.2: Two Libraries (Challenging)

Suppose you're trying to integrate two modules from two different sources. Each module has its own logging approach. Their APIs are

System A: Calls to `LogFile.log` are sprinkled throughout the code.

```
LogFile.setLog("file.log")
LogFile.log(:info, "some message")
Logfile.log(:error, "another message")
# or use :warn or :fatal
```

System B: Any object that wants to write values to the log file will hold an instance of Log.

```
LogFacility.setOutput('file2.log')
@logger = LogFacility.makeLog('id')

@logger.informational('yet another message')
# all forms take optional exception
@logger.warning('msg', exception)

@logger.fatal('fatal message')
```

Your long-term goal is to move to the standard Logger facility in Ruby 1.8, but your environment doesn't support that yet.

   A. What overall approach would you use to harmonize these classes with where you want to go? (Make sure to address the Ruby 1.8 concern.)

   B. Create a simple test for each logger, and implement the logger with the simplest approach you can.

   C. Describe how to harmonize the classes so you can eliminate one of them. (Don't worry about the Ruby 1.8 future yet.)

See page 225 for solution ideas.

Exercise 8.3: Environment Variables

```
module Timer
  def times(env)
    value_s = env['interval']
    if value_s == nil
      raise "interval missing"
    end
    value = Integer(value_s)

    if value <= 0
      raise "interval should be > 0"
    end
    check_interval = value

    value_s = env['duration']
    raise "duration missing" if value_s.nil?
    value = Integer(value_s)
```

```
  if value <= 0
   raise "duration should be > 0"
  end
  if (value % check_interval) != 0
   raise "duration should be multiple of interval"
  end
  monitor_time = value

  value_s = env['departure']
  if value_s.nil?
   raise "departure missing"
  end
  value = Integer(value_s)
  raise "departure should be > 0" if value <= 0
  if (value % check_interval) != 0
   raise "departure should be multiple of interval"
  end
  departure_offset = value
  [check_interval, monitor_time, departure_offset]
 end
end
```

A. How would you handle the duplication?

See page 226 for solution ideas.

Exercise 8.4: Template

```
module Template
  def template(source_template, req_id)
    template = String.new(source_template)

    # Substitute for %CODE%
    template_split_begin = template.index("%CODE%")
    template_split_end = template_split_begin + 6
    template_part_one =
     String.new(template[0..(template_split_begin-1)])
    template_part_two =
     String.new(template[template_split_end..template.length])
    code = String.new(req_id)
    template =
     String.new(template_part_one + code + template_part_two)
```

```
    # Substitute for %ALTCODE%
    template_split_begin = template.index("%ALTCODE%")
    template_split_end = template_split_begin + 9
    template_part_one =
      String.new(template[0..(template_split_begin-1)])
    template_part_two =
      String.new(template[template_split_end..template.length])
    altcode = code[0..4] + "-" + code[5..7]
    puts template_part_one + altcode + template_part_two
  end
end
```

A. What duplication do you see?

B. What would you do to remove the duplication?

C. One piece that repeats is a structure of the form `String.new(something)`. What does this code do? Is it necessary?

See page 227 for solution ideas.

Exercise 8.5: Duplicate Observed Data (Challenging)

The refactoring *Duplicate Observed Data* works like this: If you have domain data in a widget, move the domain data to a new domain class, and set up an observer so that the widget is notified of any changes to it.

  Thus, we started with a situation where data was in one place (the widget). We have not only duplicated it (holding it in both the widget and the domain object), but we've also added a need for synchronization between two objects.

A. Why is this duplication considered acceptable (even desirable)? (Hint: Your answer should touch on the Observer or Model-View-Controller patterns.)

B. What are the performance implications of this approach?

See page 227 for solution ideas.

Exercise 8.6: Ruby Libraries

A. The Ruby core and standard libraries have several places where there is duplication. Describe some examples of this. They might be at a low, medium, or high
   level.

B. Why does this duplication exist? Is it worth it?

See page 228 for solution ideas.

Exercise 8.7: Points

Suppose you see these two classes (bird.rb and button.rb):

```ruby
# bird.rb
require 'point.rb'

class Bird
  attr_accessor :location

  def initialize max_x, max_y
    @@max_x = max_x
    @@max_y = max_y
    @location = Point.new 0, 0
  end

  def move_by(point)
    @location.x = (@location.x + point.x) % @@max_x
    @location.y = (@location.y + point.y) % @@max_y
  end
end


#button.rb
require 'point.rb'

class Button
  attr_accessor :name
  attr_accessor :x, :y

  def initialize name, x_limit, y_limit
    @name = name
    @xmax = x_limit
    @ymax = y_limit
```

```
    @x = 0
    @y = 0
  end
  def move_to(x, y)
    @x = limit(x, @xmax)
    @y = limit(y, @ymax)
  end

private
  def limit(v, vmax)
    result = v
    while result >= vmax
      result -= vmax
    end
    while result < 0
      result += vmax
    end
    result
  end
end
```

A. What is the duplication?

B. What could you do to eliminate duplication in these two classes?

C. Sometimes, two versions of duplicated code are similar, but one has fixed a bug and the other hasn't. How can refactoring help you in this situation?

See page 229 for solution ideas.

Exercise 8.8: XML Report

Suppose we're writing a script to convert a textual report from a mainframe and reformat it into XML. Some of our current code looks like this:

```
class ReportRow
  def to_xml
    result = "<row>\n"
    @columns.each do |col|
      result += col.print + "\n"
    end
    return result + "</row>"
  end
end
```

```
class ReportColumn
  def print
    "<column>#{@value.modulo(100)}</column>"
  end
end
```

A. Identify the duplication. Are there any other smells in this code?

B. Devise at least two different approaches to removing the duplication. What are the relative pros and cons of each?

C. Try both approaches. Which was more difficult? Does this affect your assessment of the pros and cons?

See page 229 for solution ideas.

CHAPTER 9

Conditional Logic

It's natural that object-oriented programming is focused on objects and their relationships, but the code within an object is important too. Classic books like Jon Bentley's *Programming Pearls* [6] and *More Programming Pearls* [7] or Brian Kernighan and P. J. Plauger's *The Elements of Programming Style* [18] can help inspire you to write good, clean code.

Conditional logic is often the trickiest part of such code.

- It's hard to reason about, since we have to consider multiple paths through the code.
- It's tempting to add special-case handling rather than develop the general case.
- Conditional logic sometimes is used as a weak substitute for object-oriented mechanisms.

In this chapter we'll cover the following smells:

- **Nil Check,** in which `nil` is used to signal something special
- **Special Case,** in which one scenario is handled differently than the rest
- **Complicated Boolean Expression,** in which the logic is impenetrable
- **Control Coupling,** in which the caller decides which path a method should take
- **Simulated Polymorphism,** in which duck-typing is hand-coded using conditionals

Nil Check

What to Look For

- There are repeated occurrences of `if xxx.nil?` or `if xxx == nil`, especially in guard clauses at the top of methods and blocks.

Why This Is a Problem

⋈ **Duplication:** The multiple identical queries are duplication, with all the problems that brings.

↝ **Flexibility:** When `nil` is a possible value, it implies that every client must be careful to make this check to avoid a latent bug.

When to Leave It

If the **Nil Check** occurs in only one place (e.g., in a Factory Method), it is usually not worth the effort to create a separate Null Object.

Watch out for a case where `nil` means two or more different things in different contexts. (You may be able to support this with different Null Objects.)

How It Got This Way

A developer decided, "We'll use `nil` to mean the default." This may have avoided the need to initialize certain variables, or it may have been an afterthought for an unexpected case. The **Nil Check** may have been introduced to work around a defect (without addressing the underlying cause).

What to Do

Try to restrict **Nil Checks** to interface boundaries. Ensure that only valid objects are used in the bulk of the system to avoid the need for these checks.

- If there's a reasonable default value, use that.
- You may find the Ruby idiom `variable = value || default` useful at the point where you set the value. (If `value` is nil, it sets the variable to the default.)
- Otherwise, *Introduce Null Object* creates a default object that you explicitly use. You may find `method_missing` useful in this.

However, Null Objects need to have safe behavior for the methods they provide. They often act as identity objects (as 0 does relative to addition). If you can't define a safe behavior for each method, you may not be able to use a Null Object.

What to Look for Next

⋈ **Duplication:** A single "missing object" defect may have spawned identical defensive code blocks throughout the application; those can be removed.

▽ **Size:** Removing the now-extraneous **Nil Checks** will make the code easier to read and digest.

◎ **Abstraction:** It may turn out that all of the code to handle a certain special case can be brought together into a single Null Object class, which then comes to represent a genuine behavioral abstraction from the application's domain.

Special Case

What to Look For

- Complex `if` statements.
- Guard clauses—checks for particular values before doing work (especially comparisons to constants).

Why This Is a Problem

◁ **Communication:** A **Special Case** increases the amount the reader has to hold in his head while attempting to understand a code fragment.

When to Leave It

In a recursive algorithm there are always one or more base cases that will stop the recursion; you can't expect to eliminate these. And sometimes an `if` or `unless` clause is just the simplest way to do something.

How It Got This Way

Sometimes, introducing a **Special Case** was the easiest way to get to the green bar. Other times, a guard clause may have been introduced to defend against an unruly caller, or while simplifying a **Complicated Boolean Expression** during refactoring.

What to Do

- If the conditionals are taking the place of polymorphism, *Replace Conditional with Polymorphism.* You may find things become more clear if you first use *Extract Method* on the clauses.
- If the `if` and `else` clauses are similar enough, you may be able to rewrite them so that the same code fragment can generate the proper results for each case; then the conditional can be eliminated.
- If you have a defensive guard clause, try pushing it up into the method's callers (see **Control Coupling** for detailed mechanics).

What to Look for Next

⋈ **Duplication:** Removal of a special case may render the code similar to another fragment elsewhere or reveal a common structure that was previously obscured.

- **Simplicity:** Pushing guard clauses up the call tree often reveals a single cause for multiple defensive conditional clauses. Catch the **Special Case** where it arises, or look for ways to prevent that case completely.

Complicated Boolean Expression

What to Look For

- Code has complex conditions involving `and`, `or`, and `not`.

Why This Is a Problem

◁ **Communication:** Any code that requires the reader to resort to dry runs or drawing truth tables is going to slow everyone who encounters it.

⤳ **Flexibility:** A complex Boolean expression can be a "no-go area," discouraging developers from changing the code around it.

When to Leave It

You may be able to find other ways to simplify the expressions, or you may find that the rewritten expression communicates less than original.

How It Got This Way

The code may have been complicated from the beginning, or it may have picked up additional conditions along the way. Sometimes code like this has been directly translated from a textbook calculation or formula.

What to Do

- Flip the sense:

  `if !a` becomes `unless a`

  and

  `unless !a` becomes `if a`

- Apply DeMorgan's Law:

  `!(a && b)` becomes `(!a) || (!b)`

  and

  `!(a || b)` becomes `(!a) && (!b)`

  You may find that some variables will communicate better if they change names to reflect their flipped sense.

- Use *Introduce Explaining Variable* to make each clause clearer.
- Use guard clauses to peel off certain conditions; the remaining clauses get simpler.
- *Decompose Conditional* pulls each part into its own method.

What to Look for Next

◁ **Communication:** Improved readability may expose previously undiscovered defects in the code.

↝ **Flexibility:** If you peeled the condition apart to create one or more guard clauses, check whether you now have a **Nil Check** or a **Special Case**.

Control Coupling

What to Look For

- A method or block checks the value of a parameter in order to decide which execution path to take.
- A method's name includes a word such as "or."

Why This Is a Problem

⋈ **Duplication: Control Coupling** is a kind of duplication, because the caller already knows which path should be taken.

⤳ **Flexibility:** The caller and callee are coupled together—any change to the possible values of the controlling parameter must be reflected on both sides.

- **Simplicity:** The called method is probably also a **Greedy Method**, because it includes at least two different code paths.

How It Got This Way

Sometimes we want to modify a method's behavior slightly, but we don't want to lose the original behavior, so we add a parameter and use it to vary the method's course.

What to Do

1. Use *Extract Method* to strip the controlled method down to the bare skeleton.
2. Then use *Inline Method* to push the responsibility back up to the caller(s).
3. Repeat all the way up the call stack to the source of the control value.

What to Look for Next

⋈ **Duplication:** If the control parameter was passed by more than one caller, the *Inline Method* step (mentioned in the preceding section) will have introduced some duplication; remove it as you go.

▽ **Size:** After the dust has settled, check whether any of the *Inline Method* steps left behind a **Lazy Class**.

◎ **Abstraction:** When you've found the source(s) of the control variable, you probably now have a case of **Simulated Polymorphism**.

Simulated Polymorphism

What to Look For

- Code uses a `case` statement (especially on a type field).
- Code has several `if` statements in a row (especially if they're comparing against the same value).
- Code uses `instance_of?`, `kind_of?`, `is_a?`, or `===` to decide what type it's working with.
- Multiple conditionals in different places test the same value.

Why This Is a Problem

⤳ **Flexibility:** When the same value is tested in multiple places throughout an application, any change to the set of possible values causes many methods and classes to change. This is a major cause of both **Shotgun Surgery** and **Divergent Change**, and missing a single case could introduce defects.

◎ **Abstraction:** Tests for the type of an object may indicate that the abstraction represented by that type is not completely defined (or understood).

◁ **Communication:** Conditional code is hard to read and understand, because the reader must hold more state in his head.

When to Leave It

Sometimes—particularly at subsystem boundaries—a `case` statement is the simplest way to express the logic.

How It Got This Way

This smell is often caused by laziness in introducing new classes. The first time you need conditional behavior, you might use an `if` or `case` statement rather than a new class. It's not a big problem at this point because it only occurs once. However, if you then need another condition based on the same type code, you introduce a second case instead of fixing the lack of polymorphism.

Sometimes the lack of polymorphism is hidden behind a series of `if` statements instead of an explicit `case` statement, but the root problem is the same.

What to Do

Don't simulate polymorphism—use mechanisms built into the programming language.

- If a case statement on the same condition occurs in several places, it is often using a type code; replace this with the polymorphism built into objects. It takes a series of refactorings to make this change:

  1. *Extract Method.* Pull out the code for each branch.

  2. *Move Method.* Move related code onto the right class.

  3. *Replace Type Code with Subclass* or *Replace Type Code with State/Strategy.* Set up the inheritance structure.

  4. *Replace Conditional with Polymorphism.* Eliminate the conditionals.

- If the conditions occur within a single class, you might be able to replace the conditional logic via *Replace Parameter with Explicit Methods* or *Introduce Null Object.*

What to Look for Next

◁ **Communication:** Creating classes to bring together the conditional branches gives names to these abstractions. Review the names of these and related classes.

⋈ **Duplication:** These refactorings often bring together branches from different conditionals into a single new class. Review the new class for **Duplicated Code** and inconsistency smells among its methods.

Exercises

Exercise 9.1: Null Object

Look again at the code in Exercise 5.2.

A. Some of the **Nil Checks** are checks for nil strings. One approach would be to use empty strings instead. What are the downsides of this approach (taking into account the test code and all the other client classes you don't see here)?

B. What's another approach to this problem?

C. Extract a `Bin` class, and use *Introduce Null Object*.

See page 230 for solution ideas.

Exercise 9.2: Conditional Expression

Consider this code fragment:

```
if !((score > 700) ||
    ((income >= 40000) && (income <= 100000) &&
    authorized && (score > 500)) ||
    (income > 100000))
    reject
else
    accept
end
```

A. Apply DeMorgan's Law to simplify this as much as possible.

B. Starting from the original, rewrite the condition by introducing explaining variables.

C. Starting from the original again, flip the `if` and `else` clauses, then break it into several `if` clauses. (You'll call `accept()` in three different places.)

D. Use *Consolidate Conditional Expression* by extracting a method to compute the condition.

E. Which approach was the simplest? The clearest? Can you combine the techniques?

F. Describe the conditions in table form. The rows and columns should be based on three variables: one for the three score ranges, one for the income ranges, and one for the authorized flag. The cells should say either "accept" or "reject."

See page 230 for solution ideas.

Exercise 9.3: Case Statement

Consider this code:

```
def print_it(op)
    case op.type
    when '+'
         out = "push"
    when '-'
         out = "pop"
    when '@'
         out = "top"
    else
         out = "unknown"
    end
    puts "operation = #{out}"
end

def do_it(op, stack, item)
    case op.type
    when '+'
         stack.push(item)
    when '-'
         stack.pop
    end
end
```

A. What would you do?

B. Suggest some places in a typical application where a case statement might not be a bad smell.

See page 231 for solution ideas.

Exercise 9.4: Guard Clauses (Challenging)

Find some code you wrote recently in which some methods have defensive guard clauses.

A. Using the algorithm suggested under **Control Coupling,** push the guards as far as possible up the call tree.

B. What happens when you hit an API or callback interface? What forces prevent or permit you to continue the refactoring?

C. Does your application now have more or fewer conditional checks? Does the resulting code indicate any missing abstractions?

D. The methods that were originally "guarded" are now unprotected. Are they (and their enclosing classes) better or worse off for that?

Exercise 9.5: Factory Method (Challenging)

Consider these classes:

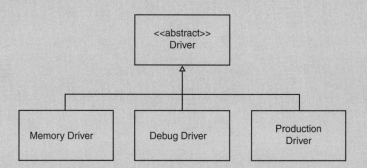

Now imagine that we want to hide the choice of driver from the rest of the application, so we introduce a Factory class that looks something like this:

```
USE_MEMORY_DRIVER = 1
USE_DEBUG_DRIVER = 2
USE_PRODUCTION_DRIVER = 3
class DriverFactory
  def initialize(type)
    @type = type
  end

  def make_driver
    #...
  end
end
```

A. Write code for the factory according to the implied design. Note: One of the three constants is passed to the `DriverFactory`'s constructor; this determines what type of driver will be returned by `make_driver`.

B. Your code probably includes a `case` statement or a series of `if`s. Is this conditional logic justified? What other smells do you see in this design?

C. Redesign `DriverFactory` so that the constants and conditionals are no longer required.

D. Your code no longer mentions the types explicitly. What are some advantages to that?

E. What are some disadvantages to this new arrangement?

See page 232 for solution ideas.

CHAPTER 10

Data

Data can be defined as simple facts, divorced from information about what to do with them. "Data" has a dusty whiff about it, the old-fashioned ring of *data processing* or *data structures*.

Data is often a natural starting point for thinking about things. For example, we know we have a first name, middle name, and last name, so we create a Person class with that information. But *objects* are about *data* and *behavior* together—your code will be more robust if you organize objects by behavior.

Data-oriented objects are an opportunity. The smells in this chapter are often signs of a missing or inadequately formed class. If the data represents a good clustering, we'll usually be able to find behavior that belongs with it in a class.

In this chapter we'll cover the following smells:

- **Open Secret**, in which a domain concept's representation hasn't been encapsulated
- **Data Class**, in which a class has little or no behavior
- **Data Clump**, in which a bunch of values travel around together
- **Temporary Field**, in which an instance variable has a different lifecycle than its enclosing class

Open Secret

Sometimes, a simple data type (such as a number or string) is used to encode a value that could be a domain object in its own right. The representation of this value is exposed; clients have to decode it and enforce any business rules themselves.

(This smell was called *Primitive Obsession* in Fowler's *Refactoring* [1] but Ruby doesn't have the concept of primitives in the sense that C++ and Java do. It's the exposure of representation that's important, not the kind of item it's stored in.)

What to Look For

- Several classes or modules pass around a simple value, and they all know how to interpret it. (The classic example is a String that "represents" a phone number.)
- Several classes or modules know what data is held in each slot of an `Array` or `Hash`.

Why This Is a Problem

◁ **Communication:** The value represents a concept, often from the application domain; but as yet the concept has not been named or provided with clear semantics.

⋈ **Duplication:** A domain concept or design decision has been implemented, but knowledge of its implementation details is spread around the code. This leads to duplication of knowledge—and often of code—among the clients of this value.

• **Simplicity: Shotgun Surgery** is almost always caused by an **Open Secret**—indeed, we are often alerted to this smell by encountering **Shotgun Surgery** first.

When to Leave It

Very rarely, you may decide that fixing this smell would create dependency or performance problems.

Particularly for a `Hash` or an `Array`, you may decide that convenience outweighs any need to remove this smell.

A `Hash` may represent a simple map of values; if there's no interpretation layered over top of it, there may be less of the smell (but note that you're still exposing the implementation and there may still be a missing object).

How It Got This Way

It's easy to start with a string or numeric type, and later miss an opportunity to introduce a new class.

What to Do

- If you have a primitive whose value is interpreted by several classes, fix it as if it were a **Data Clump**.

- If you have an `Array` or a `Hash` whose "layout" is common knowledge, use *Replace Array with Object* or *Replace Hash with Object*.

What to Look for Next

⋈ **Duplication:** The class you just extracted is a **Data Class**. Look for opportunities to flesh out its behavior by reviewing its clients for **Feature Envy**. You will often find clients performing validation or formatting of the value.

◁ **Communication:** You have given a name to a domain concept; review the other names that are used around the new class.

⇝ **Flexibility:** Look for ways to push the construction of your new object backward in time, so that more parts of your application benefit from the new class's semantics and communication capabilities. If the new class is immutable and has a small set of possible or common values, consider introducing Flyweight instances.

Data Class

What to Look For

- A class consists only of trivial reader and writer methods for instance variables, maybe with a constructor to initialize them.

Why This Is a Problem

◎ **Abstraction:** Objects are intended to encapsulate both data and behavior, but a **Data Class** only has data. The clients of the class do the "heavy lifting" for the class.

⋈ **Duplication:** Multiple clients often have to do similar work.

When to Leave It

There are times when an `attr_accessor` is the simplest and best approach. For example, consider a point with `x` and `y` coordinates. The interface probably isn't going to change, and people may deal with *lots* of points. So it makes sense for a `Point` class to declare public `attr_accessor`s.

Some persistence mechanisms (e.g., ActiveRecord) rely on reflection to determine what data should be loaded or stored. Such classes may be constrained by their "data class" nature. (You can add methods, but the class tends to be centered around its data.) It is sometimes better to treat these classes as Mementos (see Gamma's *Design Patterns*), and to use another class as a layer above these persistence-only classes; that new class can benefit from all the changes described here, and it will hide the low-level classes.

How It Got This Way

It's common for classes to begin like this: You realize that some data is part of an independent object, so you extract it. In fact, the creation of a **Data Class** is a good first step in removing the **Open Secret** and **Data Clump** smells. But objects are about the commonality of *behavior*, and these objects aren't developed enough as yet to have much behavior.

What to Do

1. Use *Remove Setting Methods* for as many instance variables as you can.
2. Use *Encapsulate Collection* to remove direct access to any collection-type fields.

3. Look at each client of the object. Almost invariably, you'll find **Feature Envy** and **Inappropriate Intimacy (General Form)**—clients accessing the fields and manipulating the results when the data class could do it for them. (This is often a source of duplication, because many callers will tend to do the same things with the data.) Use *Extract Method* on the client to pull out the class-related code, then *Move Method* to pull it over to the class.

4. After doing this a while, you may find that you have several similar methods on the class. Use *Rename Method, Extract Method, Add Parameter*, or *Remove Parameter* to harmonize signatures and remove duplication.

5. Most access to the instance variables shouldn't be needed any more because the moved methods cover the real use. Use *Remove Method* to eliminate the readers and writers.

What to Look for Next

◁ **Communication:** Review the names used in this class to ensure that the methods you bring in present a consistent API to the class's clients.

⋈ **Duplication:** Where you moved methods from clients into this class, check whether those clients are now Lazy Classes and whether they now contain further Duplication.

Data Clump

What to Look For

- The same two or three items frequently appear together in classes and parameter lists.
- A group of instance variable names start or end with similar substrings.

Why This Is a Problem

⋈ **Duplication:** The recurrence of the items often means there is duplicate code spread around to handle them.

◎ **Abstraction:** There may be a missing concept, making the system harder to understand.

When to Leave It

Passing a *Whole Object* sometimes introduces a dependency you don't want (as lower-level classes get exposed to the whole new object instead of just its components). You may continue to pass in the pieces to prevent this dependency.

Very rarely, there is a measured performance problem solved by passing in the parts of the object instead of the object itself. Recognize that this is a compromise in the object model for performance. Such code is worth commenting!

How It Got This Way

The items are typically part of some other entity, but as yet no one has had the insight to realize that there's a missing class. Or, sometimes, people know the class is missing but think it's too small or unimportant to stand alone.

(Identifying these classes is often a major step toward simplifying a system, and it often helps you to generalize classes more easily.)

What to Do

- If the items are instance variables in a class, use *Extract Class* to pull them into a new class.
- If the values are together in method signatures, use *Introduce Parameter Object* to extract the new object.

What to Look for Next

◁ **Communication:** Review calls that pass around the items from the new object; look for opportunities to use *Preserve Whole Object.*

⋈ **Duplication:** Look at uses of the items; there are often opportunities to use *Move Method,* etc., to move those uses into the new object (as you would to address the **Data Class** smell).

Temporary Field

What to Look For

An instance variable is set only at certain times, and it is `nil` (or unused) at other times.

Why This Is a Problem

◎ **Abstraction:** Parts of the object change at different rates, and the class spends effort coordinating the changes. This suggests there is an implicit concept that can be brought out (with its own lifetime).

When to Leave It

It may not be worth the trouble of creating a new class if it doesn't represent a useful abstraction.

How It Got This Way

This can happen when one part of an object has an algorithm that passes around information through the instance variables rather than parameters; the instance variables are valid or used only when the algorithm is active. The fact that the instance variables are sometimes used and sometimes not suggests that there may be a missing object whose life cycle differs from that of the object holding them.

What to Do

• Use *Extract Class*, moving over the fields and any related code.

What to Look for Next

◎ **Abstraction:** The new class is likely a **Data Class**.
⋈ **Duplication:** Look for other places that embody the same concept; they may be creating duplication.

Exercises

Exercise 10.1: Alternative Representations

Imagine that the following domain concepts are classes in some application. For each, suggest two or three different ways in which its value could be represented in instance variables:

A. Money

B. Position (in a list)

C. Range

D. Social Security Number (government identification number: "123-45-6789")

E. Telephone number

F. Street Address ("123 E. Main Street")

G. ZIP (postal) code

See page 233 for solution ideas.

Exercise 10.2: Primitives and Middle Men

A. Wrapping a "primitive" object inside a new class can appear to be introducing a **Middle Man**. Why (or when) is that not the case?

B. Find some code you wrote recently in which the **Open Secret** smell is present. Fix it by wrapping the primitive inside a new class, named for the domain concept it represents. Is this new class a **Middle Man**? Why or why not?

See page 234 for solution ideas.

Exercise 10.3: Rails Accounts

We're in the early stages of developing a Rails app to manage personal checking accounts using double-entry bookkeeping. Our schema currently shows three models:

```
class CreateAccounts < ActiveRecord::Migration
  def self.up
```

```
  create_table "accounts", :force => true do |t|
    t.string "name"
    t.integer "opening_balance"
    t.datetime "created_at"
    t.datetime "updated_at"
  end

  create_table "postings", :force => true do |t|
    t.integer "amount"
    t.integer "account_id"
    t.integer "transaction_id"
    t.datetime "created_at"
    t.datetime "updated_at"
  end

  create_table "transactions", :force => true do |t|
    t.date "occurred_on"
    t.string "payee"
    t.string "reason"
    t.datetime "created_at"
    t.datetime "updated_at"
  end

end

def self.down
  drop_table :transactions
  drop_table :postings
  drop_table :accounts
end
end
```

A transaction posts a monetary amount to each of a series of accounts, where Posting is the join object representing the many-many relationship between accounts and transactions. An account can provide its (current) balance:

```
class Account < ActiveRecord::Base
  has_many :postings
  has_many :transactions, :through => :postings

  validates_presence_of :name
  validates_uniqueness_of :name
  validates_numericality_of :opening_balance

  def balance
    postings.inject(0) { |sum, i| sum + i.amount }
  end
end
```

In order to conform to double-entry bookkeeping rules, we also added some custom validation to check that each transaction posts a set of amounts that sum to zero:

```
class Transaction < ActiveRecord::Base
  has_many :postings
  has_many :accounts, :through => :postings

  validates_presence_of :payee
  validates_presence_of :reason
  validates_presence_of :occurred_on

  def validate_postings(postings)
    if postings.size < 2
      errors.add_to_base("Provide at least two postings")
    else
      bal = postings.inject(0) do |sum, po|
        sum + po['amount'].to_i
      end
      errors.add_to_base("Sum must be zero") if bal != 0
    end
  end
end
```

We have a view showing the balance of every account:

```
<h1>Account Balances</h1>
<table width="100%">
  <tr> <th> Account </th> <th> Balance </th> </tr>
<% for account in @accounts %>
  <tr>
    <td width="60%"><%= link_to account.name, account %></td>
    <td align="right"><%= to_money(account.balance) %></td>
  </tr>
<% end %>
</table>
```

We also have a view showing a statement for a single account, and another showing the details of a single transaction. Each of these views displays monetary amounts in the same way, so to DRY up our app we've written a helper method:

```
module ApplicationHelper
  def to_money(amount)
    '%0.2f' % (amount/100.0)
  end
end
```

(We didn't use the standard number_to_currency helper because we don't want currency symbols everywhere.)

A. What smell do you see, and what action would you take to remove it?

See page 234 for solution ideas.

Exercise 10.4: Long Parameter List

Consider these methods from RMagick::Draw:

```
arc(startX, startY, endX, endY, startDegrees, endDegrees)

ellipse(originX, originY, width, height, arcStart, arcEnd)

rectangle(upper_left_x, upper_left_y,
    lower_right_x, lower_right_y)
```

A. For each declaration above, is there any cluster of parameters you might reasonably group into a new object?

B. Why might those signatures have so many parameters?

See page 235 for solution ideas.

Exercise 10.5: A Counter-Argument

Consider a business application where a user enters a ZIP code (among other things), and it gets stored in a relational database. Someone argues: "It's not worth the bother of turning it into an object: When it gets written, it will just have to be turned into a primitive again." Why might it be worth creating the object in spite of the need for two conversions?

See page 235 for solution ideas.

Exercise 10.6: Editor

Consider this interface to an editor:

```
class Editor
  insert(text)
  fetch(number_of_characters_to_fetch) # -> String
  move_to(position)
  5 position                           # -> Fixnum
  # etc...
end
```

and this sequence of calls:

```
editor.insert("ba(nana)")
index_of_opening_parens = 2
editor.move_to(index_of_opening_parens)
assert_equal "(", editor.fetch(1)

editor.move_to(1)
editor.insert("x")
editor.move_to(index_of_opening_parens)
assert_equal ___, editor.fetch(1)
```

   A. Given the interface provided, what string would you expect to appear in place
      of the ___ in the final assertion?

   B. Based on the variable name `index_of_opening_parens`, what string would you
      prefer to appear? Of what use would this be?

   C. The crux of the problem is the use of a Fixnum as a position index. Suggest an
      alternative approach.

   D. Relate your solution to the Memento design pattern (from Gamma's *Design Pat-
      terns* [16]).

See page 235 for solution ideas.

Exercise 10.7: Library Classes

The built-in `Thread` class has what appears to be public instance variables (`abort_on_exception`, `priority`, etc.). What, if anything, do these reveal about `Thread`'s
internal design?

See page 236 for solution ideas.

Exercise 10.8: Hidden State

The standard library classes `Set` and `DateTime` are encapsulated such that access to
their state is only through methods.

   A. Propose at least two internal representations for each class.

B. Ruby provides no way to directly access an instance variable from outside a class.
(You have to define a method if you want to let a client change it.) How does this
promote the ability of a class to be immutable?

C. How does having no direct access to instance variables promote the design of
efficient classes?

See page 236 for solution ideas.

Exercise 10.9: Proper Names

Consider the following class:

```
Person = Struct.new('Person', :last, :first, :middle)
```

Its clients are shown in one file for convenience; imagine them as nontest methods
in separate client classes:

```
require 'stringio'
require 'test/unit'

require 'person'

class PersonClient < Test::Unit::TestCase

  def client1(out, person)
   out.write(person.first)
   out.write(" ")
   if person.middle != nil
     out.write(person.middle)
     out.write(" ")
   end
   out.write(person.last)
  end

  def client2(person)
   result = person.last + ", " + person.first
   if (person.middle != nil)
     result += " " + person.middle
   end
   return result
  end

  def client3(out, person)
   out.write(person.last)
   out.write(", ")
   out.write(person.first)
```

```
    if (person.middle != nil)
      out.write(" ")
      out.write(person.middle)
    end
  end

  def client4(person)
    return person.last + ", " +
        person.first +
        ((person.middle == nil) ? "" : " " + person.middle)
  end

  def test_clients
    bobSmith = Person.new("Smith", "Bob", nil)
    jennyJJones = Person.new("Jones", "Jenny", "J")

    out = StringIO.new
    client1(out, bobSmith)
    assert_equal("Bob Smith", out.string)

    out = StringIO.new
    client1(out, jennyJJones)
    assert_equal("Jenny J Jones", out.string)

    assert_equal("Smith, Bob", client2(bobSmith))
    assert_equal("Jones, Jenny J", client2(jennyJJones))

    out = StringIO.new
    client3(out, bobSmith)
    assert_equal("Smith, Bob", out.string)

    out = StringIO.new
    client3(out, jennyJJones)
    assert_equal("Jones, Jenny J", out.string)

    assert_equal("Smith, Bob", client4(bobSmith))
    assert_equal("Jones, Jenny J", client4(jennyJJones))
  end
end
```

A. What smell is represented by `Person`?

B. Using the clients you have, remove the smell.

C. There's a new requirement to support people with only one name (say, Cher or Madonna), or someone with several words in their last name (Oscar de los

Santos) or multiple last names (Jerry Johnson Smith). Compare the difficulty of
this change before and after your refactoring in the previous part.

See page 236 for solution ideas.

Exercise 10.10: Checkpoints

We're developing a very simple transaction mechanism, based on the following
module that allows us to checkpoint any object's state:

```
module Checkpoint
  def checkpoint
    @state = var_values
  end

  def var_values
    result = {}
    instance_variables.each do |var|
      result[var] = instance_variable_get var
    end
    result
  end

  def changes
    var_values.reject { |k,v| k == "@state" || @state[k] == v }
  end

end

class Object
    include Checkpoint
end

require 'test/unit'
require 'checkpoint'

class Customer
  attr_reader :first, :last, :ssn

  def initialize(first, last, ssn)
    @first, @last, @ssn = first, last, ssn
  end
```

```
    def marries(other)
      @last = other.last
    end
  end

  class CheckpointTest < Test::Unit::TestCase
    def test_one_variable_changed
      martha = Customer.new "Martha", "Jones", "12-345-6789"
      jack = Customer.new "Jack", "Harkness", "97-865-4321"
      martha.checkpoint
      martha.marries(jack)
      assert_equal({"@last" => "Harkness"}, martha.changes)
    end
  end
```

A. What smell do you see in the `Checkpoint` module?

B. Redesign the code to remove that smell.

C. Have you improved the code? Was it worth the effort?

See page 237 for solution ideas.

CHAPTER 11

Inheritance

The relationship between a class and its subclass often starts being simple but gets more complicated over time. A subclass often depends on its parent more intimately than does a separate class, but it can go too far.

A key challenge is deciding what a class *is* (behaves like) versus what a class *has* or *knows*. A class structure often starts with inheritance and moves to a more compositional style over time.

In this chapter we'll cover the following smells:

- **Implementation Inheritance**, in which subclassing is used purely to reuse code
- **Refused Bequest**, in which a subclass isn't substitutable for its superclass
- **Inappropriate Intimacy (Subclass Form)**, in which a subclass is tangled up in its superclass's implementation details
- **Lazy Class**, in which a class doesn't do much

Implementation Inheritance

What to Look For

- Inheritance between two classes doesn't represent an *is-a* relationship (similarity of behavior—i.e., substitutability).
- Instances of the subclass are never passed as substitutes for instances of the parent.
- A subclass uses or publishes only a subset of the behavior it inherits from its superclass. (See also **Refused Bequest**.)

Why This Is a Problem

◁ **Communication:** An inheritance relationship is likely to be read as an intention for the subclass to be *substitutable* for the parent. If that isn't the case—if the relationship exists only to allow the subclass to borrow code—then the design is being miscommunicated. Readers of this code, and designers of client classes, may make incorrect decisions by assuming that the inheritance relationship means more than was intended.

◎ **Abstraction:** The public interface of the subclass inappropriately reveals things about how the class is implemented.

⤳ **Flexibility:** Inheritance is the strongest kind of relationship between two classes, and creates a coupling that can restrict change or be difficult to break. Use inheritance sparingly, as Ruby provides more than enough other ways to share object behavior. Don't waste your one permitted superclass when you could use a delegate or a mix-in instead.

When to Leave It

This is not a strong smell, and you may decide that it just isn't serious enough to fix.

How It Got This Way

Often, creating an inheritance relationship is the quickest way to borrow code from a class that already exists.

What to Do

- If the inherited methods don't need to be public, use *Replace Inheritance with Delegation*. If only a subset of the behavior of the parent class is used, consider *Extract*

Class first and have both parent and child classes delegate to the new class, or perhaps the child class should inherit from the new class.

- If (some of) the inherited methods do need to be public on the subclass, use *Extract Module* to make them shareable and then delete the inheritance relationship. Alternatively, use *Replace Inheritance with Delegation* and reimplement the child class to act as a **Middle Man** for those methods.

What to Look for Next

◁ **Communication:** Removing unwanted inherited methods gives the class's public interface a shake-up. Look through the whole class to check for **Inconsistent Names**. Also look through the class or module you extracted, checking for naming smells (see Chapter 6, "Names," for a list of these).

- **Simplicity:** You may find that other implementation decisions depended on, or were related to, the one you have just fixed. In particular, look through both original classes for examples of **Feature Envy** in relation to the extracted class or module.

Refused Bequest

What to Look For

- **Explicit Refusal:** The subclass undefines an inherited method, makes an inherited method private, or makes it throw an exception when it is called.
- **Implicit Refusal:** A method inherited from the parent class just doesn't work for instances of the subclass.
- An inheritance relationship between two classes doesn't make sense; the subclass just isn't an example of the parent.

Why This Is a Problem

- **Simplicity:** Rejecting a parent's method violates the Liskov Substitution Principle (LSP). The refusal of the subclass to implement an inherited method means that all of its clients must cope with that refusal in some way.
- ⋈ **Duplication:** The clients need to know which class they are dealing with, so that they know whether they can safely invoke the refused method.
- ⤳ **Flexibility:** We have pushed one of the subclass's responsibilities out into other classes, which will hamper future change.

When to Leave It

If the inherited method was refused in order to prevent a **Combinatorial Explosion**, you may decide to live with the smell.

    If you leave this smell in place, move to an explicit refusal by having the subclass raise an exception when a parent method is refused. If you just leave it implicit, you can get strange behavior that is difficult to track down.

How It Got This Way

There may be a conscious decision to let subclasses deny use of some features to prevent an explosion of types for all feature combinations. More often, it's just a lazy borrowing of parts of the parent's implementation.

What to Do

- First, check if this is actually a disguised case of **Implementation Inheritance**; if so, fix that smell first.

- If there's no reason to share a class relationship, then use *Replace Inheritance with Delegation.*

- If the parent-child relationship *does* make sense, look through their clients to find places where the refused method is called. If you find conditional logic (e.g., **Special Case**) that copes with the refusal, look for ways to implement the refused method by pushing the clients' response into the refusing class. This may involve *Move Method* and/or *Introduce Null Object.* Look through Chapter 9, "Conditional Logic," for more ideas.

- Alternatively, look for ways to reorganize the inheritance relationship. For example (see Figure 11.1), you could create a new subclass C via *Extract Subclass* and use *Push Down Method* to move the refused behavior into it. Then change clients of the refused method to be clients of the new class.

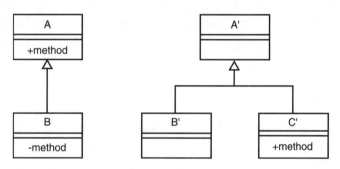

Figure 11.1 Rearranging the Hierarchy

What to Look for Next

◁ **Communication:** Fixing **Refused Bequest** will improve the way your classes communicate your design. Look again at these classes and their clients for **Uncommunicative Names** that could now be simplified or cleaned up.

• **Simplicity:** Reorganizing your classes so that they always respect the Liskov Substitution Principle will likely simplify their clients. (LSP requires that subclass instances be substitutable.) Look through all uses of the refused method for Special Cases and other signs of coping with broken polymorphism; you may now find those clients can be simplified.

↯ **Testability:** Tests are clients too. Fixing a refused method can reduce the number of cases you need to test, so check your tests for cases that now collapse or disappear.

Inappropriate Intimacy (Subclass Form)

What to Look For

- A class makes use of the implementation details of its superclass.

  (There is a related form of inappropriate intimacy between separate classes; see **Inappropriate Intimacy (General Form)** in Chapter 12, "Responsibility.")

Why This Is a Problem

⇝ **Flexibility:** If implementation details of the superclass change, the consequences could propagate to the subclass.

• **Simplicity:** If the semantics or behavior of the superclass change without affecting the types at the interface, we may introduce subtle defects in its subclasses.

  This problem is more serious between unrelated classes than between a parent and child.

How It Got This Way

It's natural that a superclass and its subclasses be more coupled together than two strangers. Sometimes it just goes too far.

What to Do

- First, check if this is also a case of **Implementation Inheritance**; if so, fix that smell first.
- If the parent can define a general algorithm that the children can plug into, then use *Form Template Method*.
- If the parent and child need to be even more decoupled, then use *Replace Inheritance with Delegation*.

What to Look for Next

◁ **Communication:** You may now have created a better abstraction by documenting the true interface of the superclass. Review the names it uses for consistency.

⋈ **Duplication:** If several subclasses had to perform the same set of actions, moving them onto the superclass can open up opportunities to simplify the subclasses too.

Lazy Class

What to Look For

- A class isn't doing much—its parents, children, or clients seem to be doing all the associated work—and there isn't enough behavior left in the class to justify its continued existence.

Lazy Class is a close relative of **Dead Code**.

Why This Is a Problem

- **Simplicity:** Every additional class in the application represents something extra to understand, and extra code to navigate while following a flow.
- ◁ **Communication:** A **Lazy Class** also occupies one of the names in your domain space, without paying for that usage.

When to Leave It

Sometimes, a **Lazy Class** is present to communicate intent. You may have to balance communication versus simplicity in your design; and when communication wins, leave the **Lazy Class** in place.

Other times, a class that appears to be lazy exists as part of the scaffolding for a framework. You could tidy it up, or leave it in place for compatibility.

How It Got This Way

Typically, all the class's responsibilities were moved to other places in the course of refactoring. Sometimes, the class was created in anticipation of some grand design that never quite materialized. Certain generators for Ruby on Rails create **Lazy Class**es to serve as hooks or placeholders for idioms you may or may not use in your application.

What to Do

- If parents or children of the class seem like the right place for the class' behavior, fold it into one of them via *Collapse Hierarchy*.
- Otherwise, fold its behavior into its caller via *Inline Class*.

What to Look for Next

⋈ **Duplication:** After the behavior of the **Lazy Class** has been folded into another class, look for **Duplicated Code** and **Dead Code** within that receiving class.

• **Simplicity:** The **Lazy Class** muddied the paths of communication between its own clients and suppliers. These classes may now be related to each other directly, so you should examine the amended methods looking for **Feature Envy** and **Utility Functions**.

Exercises

Exercise 11.1: ArrayQueue

Consider this class:

```ruby
class ArrayQueue < Array

  def add_rear(s)
    self << s
  end

  def remove_front
    self.delete_at(0)
  end
end
```

and these tests:

```ruby
require 'array_queue'
require 'test/unit'

class ArrayQueueTest < Test::Unit::TestCase
  def test_queue_invariant
    q = ArrayQueue.new
    q.add_rear("E1")
    q.add_rear("E2")
    assert_equal("E1", q.remove_front)
    assert_equal("E2", q.remove_front)
    assert_equal(0, q.length)
  end
end
```

A. What smell is in the design of `ArrayQueue`?

B. Refactor the code to remove the smell.

See page 237 for solution ideas.

Exercise 11.2: Relationships

For each of these three mechanisms for code reuse in Ruby—inheritance, delegation, and module inclusion—place a check in the table where each mechanism helps to support the corresponding quality in our software:

	Inheritance	Delegation	Module Inclusion
Flexibility			
Communication			
Testability			

See page 237 for solution ideas.

Exercise 11.3: Read-Only Documents (Challenging)

Consider the following two classes:

```
class Document
  attr_reader :numpages
  attr_writer :title, :author
  def delete(pos, length) ...
  def find(regex) ...
  def format(printer) ...
  def insert(pos, text) ...
end

class ReadonlyDocument < Document
  undef :delete, :insert, :title=, :author=
end
```

A. Suggest at least three ways to address this Refused Bequest.

B. Evaluate your candidate solutions: Which approach feels most natural? Which offers the most long-term flexibility?

See page 237 for solution ideas.

Exercise 11.4: Inheritance Survey (Challenging)

A. Look through your code and find every inheritance relationship you defined. Classify each as *Implementation Inheritance, Subclassing,* or a mixture of both.

B. Refactor to eliminate every method that doesn't need to be inherited by a subclass.

CHAPTER 12

Responsibility

It's hard to get the right balance of responsibility between objects. One of the beauties of refactoring is that it lets us experiment with different ideas in a way that lets us safely change our minds.

There are tools we can use to help us decide how our objects should work together, such as design patterns and CRC cards (see "A Laboratory for Teaching Object-Oriented Thinking" [5]).

Refactorings are often reversible, and they may trade off between two good things. A good example of this is **Message Chain** versus **Middle Man**. Sometimes there's a way to improve both smells at the same time, but many times it's a balancing act between them.

In this chapter we'll cover the following smells:

- **Feature Envy**, in which an object is peppered with requests from another code fragment

- **Utility Function**, in which a method belongs somewhere else

- **Global Variable**, in which a global variable is used

- **Inappropriate Intimacy (General Form)**, in which a class depends on implementation details of another class

- **Message Chain**, in which a method digs into the structure of another group of objects

- **Middle Man**, in which an object merely delegates to another

- **Greedy Module**, in which a class or module has more than one responsibility

Feature Envy

What to Look For

- A code fragment references another object more often than it references itself.
- Several clients do the same series of manipulations on a particular type of object.

Why This Is a Problem

◁ **Communication:** Code that "belongs" on one class but is located in another can be hard to find and may upset the *System of Names* in the host class.

⤳ **Flexibility:** A code fragment that is in the wrong class creates couplings that may not be natural within the application's domain and a loss of cohesion in the unwilling host class; **Shotgun Surgery** and **Divergent Change** often occur as a consequence.

⋈ **Duplication:** Existing functionality that is difficult to find is also easy to miss, which in turn may lead to it being written more than once.

When to Leave It

Sometimes behavior is intentionally put on the "wrong" class. For example, some design patterns, such as Strategy or Visitor, pull behavior to a separate class so it can be independently changed. If you put it back, with *Move Method* you can end up putting things together that should change separately.

How It Got This Way

Wherever you have a **Data Class** you will probably also have **Feature Envy**, but you can see it for any class and its clients.

What to Do

1. If the envious code fragment is not isolated, use *Extract Method* to pull it into its own method.
2. If the envious method makes no references to `self` or `self.class`, see **Utility Function**.
3. Look for the class of the object that is referenced most and use *Move Method* to put the actions on the correct class.

What to Look for Next

⋈ **Duplication:** If you moved code in order to alleviate duplication in a number of clients, look again at those clients for further opportunities to simplify.

◁ **Communication:** Review the names in the receiving class for consistency.

Utility Function

What to Look For

- An instance method has no dependency on the state of the instance.

Why This Is a Problem

A **Utility Function** is an extreme kind of **Feature Envy**, and should be fixed for much the same reasons:

- ◎ **Abstraction: Utility Functions** often indicate that part of the domain has not been named and expressed as objects.
- ↝ **Flexibility:** A method that is in the wrong class creates couplings that may not be natural within the application's domain and a loss of cohesion in the unwilling host class; **Shotgun Surgery** and **Divergent Change** often occur as a consequence.
- ⋈ **Duplication:** Existing functionality that is difficult to find is also easy to miss, which in turn may lead to it being written more than once.

When to Leave It

A **Utility Function** is sometimes the most direct way of describing a design. For example, a Factory may best be expressed using class methods.

How It Got This Way

Sometimes there just doesn't seem anywhere suitable to put the new method you're writing, so you "temporarily" add it to an existing class, or create a new Utilities class to hold it. This often arises from thinking of classes as "containers of functions" rather than as descriptions of the behavior of objects.

Sometimes other refactorings—notably *Extract Method*—leave behind a stub that now has nothing to do with the object in which it sits.

What to Do

- As a minimum, document the fact that this is a **Utility Function** by converting it to being a class method.
- Look at the method's parameters; if one is used significantly more than the others, or if one looks like the "right" home, use *Move Method* to move the method onto that parameter's class.

- If a group of **Utility Functions** looks as if they belong together—for example, if they have one or more common parameters—consider using *Extract Class* and *Move Method* to create a new home for them.

What to Look for Next

◁ **Communication:** Moving code to where it fits logically within the domain can help you find it again later.

⋈ **Duplication:** If several clients had to perform the same set of actions, moving them onto the supplier class can open up opportunities to simplify the clients too.

Global Variable

What to Look For

- Your code uses a global variable, other than one predefined by Ruby itself.

Why This Is a Problem

⤳ **Flexibility:** Global variables make it easy for one part of the system to accidentally depend on another part of the system. The system is more prone to problems where changing something over here breaks something over there. Furthermore, global variables aren't thread safe, so they increase the risk of obscure bugs.

↯ **Testability:** Global variables can make it hard to set up tests: the context of the test includes all global state.

When to Leave It

A global variable can be the simplest way to go in simple scripting. But as soon as you begin to define your own domain classes it's best to eliminate any **Global Variables**.

How It Got This Way

The easiest way to establish communication between parts of a program is to introduce a **Global Variable**.

What to Do

- Use *Add Parameter* to give methods access to the value, so that the application accesses the global variable directly at only the highest level. Then you have a choice: Move the global to the class where it belongs and hand out the instance of that class, or create a Registry of some sort and hand out the value from the registry.

What to Look for Next

◎ **Abstraction:** Look for **Data Clumps** involving the new parameter. Are there other global variables, or objects, that travel with this one?

⋈ **Duplication:** As you make the changes to replace the global access by a method parameter, look out for code fragments that use the parameter in similar ways. Treat the duplication as you find it.

Inappropriate Intimacy (General Form)

What to Look For

- One class uses or changes "internal" (should-be-private) parts of another class.

- One class depends on implementation details of another class.

- Code uses `instance_variables` or `instance_variable_get` to dig inside another object.

(There is a related form of inappropriate intimacy between subclass and superclass; .see **Inappropriate Intimacy (Subclass Form)** in Chapter 11, "Inheritance.")

Why This Is a Problem

⤳ **Flexibility:** If implementation details of the "violated" class change, the consequences could propagate to the client.

• **Simplicity:** If the semantics or behavior of the "violated" class change, but don't affect the types at the interface, we may introduce subtle defects in its clients.

◎ **Abstraction:** There may be a missing concept embedded in the interaction between the existing classes.

⋈ **Duplication:** Several client classes may duplicate code by accessing internals in similar ways.

When to Leave It

Digging into another object's state is sometimes the simplest way to get something done. It is often necessary in order to implement a generic data transfer mechanism—for example, as part of a persistence scheme or to implement views that can display arbitrary objects.

How It Got This Way

The two classes probably became intertwined a little at a time. By the time you realize there's a problem, they're tightly coupled.

What to Do

- If two independent classes are entangled, use *Move Method* and *Move Instance Variable* to put the right pieces on the right class.

- If the tangled part seems to be a missing concept or class, use *Extract Class* and *Hide Delegate* to introduce the new class.

- If a client is using Ruby's metaprogramming tools to dig into an object's state, consider using Kent Beck's Double Dispatch pattern [2] and have the "violated" object publish information instead.

- If a subclass is too coupled to its superclass, see **Inappropriate Intimacy (Subclass Form)** in Chapter 11.

What to Look for Next

◁ **Communication:** You may now have created a better abstraction by documenting the true interface of the "violated" class. Review the names it uses, for consistency.

⋈ **Duplication:** If several clients had to perform the same set of actions, moving them onto the supplier class can open up opportunities to simplify the clients too.

Message Chain

What to Look For

- You see calls of the form `a.b.c.d`.

  (This may happen directly or through intermediate results.)

Why This Is a Problem

⤳ **Flexibility:** A **Message Chain** couples the caller to the details of how to reach other objects. This coupling goes against two maxims of object-oriented programming: the *Law of Demeter* (see Exercise 12.7) and *Tell, Don't Ask*, which says that instead of *asking* for objects so you can manipulate them, you should tell them to do the manipulation for you. (Andrew Hunt and David Thomas' *The Pragmatic Programmer* [17] describes both of these rules in more detail.)

When to Leave It

Sometimes the cleanest way to construct or configure a complex of objects is to use a Cascade (Beck, *Smalltalk Best Practice Patterns* [2]) or what Martin Fowler calls a Fluent Interface [13]. Domain-specific languages (DSLs) often use this approach to provide the context necessary to enable a simplified syntax; it looks as if the caller is being encouraged to build a message chain, but usually the methods all return `self`. (It's much more of a problem when the chain of calls is coupling to several different objects.)

This is a trade-off refactoring. If you apply *Hide Delegate* too much, you get to the point where everything's so busy delegating that nothing seems to be doing any actual work. Sometimes it's just easier and less confusing to call a small chain.

How It Got This Way

When you know the relationships among a group of objects, often the fastest way to a green bar during test-driven development (TDD) is to introduce a **Message Chain**.

What to Do

- If the manipulations actually belong on the target object (the one at the end of the chain), use *Extract Method* and *Move Method* to put them there.

- Part of the chain may belong on some other object; look for **Inappropriate Intimacy**.

- Use *Hide Delegate* to make the caller depend only on the object at the head of the chain. (So, rather than `a.b.c.d`, put a `d` method on the `a` object. That may require adding a `d` method to the `b` and `c` objects as well.)

What to Look for Next

⋈ **Duplication:** If several clients had to perform the same set of actions, moving them onto the supplier class can let you simplify the clients.

Middle Man

What to Look For

A class that mostly delegates its work is known as a *Middle Man:*

- Most methods of a class call the same or a similar method on another object:
  ```
  def f
    @delegate.f
  end
  ```

Why This Is a Problem

▽ **Size:** If the **Middle Man** really is superfluous, our system has one more class than it needs.

◁ **Communication:** Extra code always slows the reader, and it occupies part of the domain's namespace, possibly using names that may be useful elsewhere.

When to Leave It

Some design patterns (e.g., Adapter, Proxy, Decorator) intentionally create delegates, so **Middle Man** and **Message Chain** trade off against each other. Delegates provide a sort of façade, letting a caller remain unaware of details of messages and structures. Removing a **Middle Man** can expose clients to more information than they should know.

How It Got This Way

It could be the result of applying *Hide Delegate* to a **Message Chain**; other features may have moved out since then, leaving you with mostly delegating methods.

What to Do

- In general, use *Remove Middle Man* by having the client call the delegate directly.
- If the delegate is owned by the middle man or is immutable, the middle man has behavior to add, and the middle man can be seen as an example of the delegate, you might use *Replace Delegation with Inheritance*.

What to Look for Next

◁ **Communication:** The true relationships between remaining classes may now be easier to determine without the **Middle Man** in the way.

Greedy Module

What to Look For

- A module has more than one responsibility—for example, formatting a report as XML *and* sending it to a SOAP service.

- The fixtures for a class's unit tests are big and clumsy, or are difficult to fabricate.

- A module embodies design decisions that need to change independently or at different frequencies.

Every **Large Module** is very likely to also be a **Greedy Module**: Some clients depend on some parts, others on different parts. A **Temporary Field** is also a sure sign.

Why This Is a Problem

⤳ **Flexibility:** One of the benefits of object-oriented design is the ability to localize change. By separating an application into small, independent pieces, we improve our chances of finding and fixing defects, and of adding new features without breaking those that work already.

- **Simplicity:** A module that does too many things, or that embodies too many design decisions, is more complicated than it needs to be.

A module that does two jobs is often said to violate the *Single Responsibility Principle* (SRP); see Robert Martin's *Agile Software Development: Principles, Patterns, and Practices* [21] for a broader explanation of the SRP.

How It Got This Way

When new behavior must be added, sometimes the quickest thing to do is to weave it into existing code. Often it begins with a **Greedy Method**, and the longer it continues the easier it becomes to just add a little more.

What to Do

- Consider the approaches to dealing with a **Large Module**—they will often work here just as well.

- Look at instance variables and method parameters. If you see a **Data Clump**, use that as the basis for a new class, as described on page 112.

- If the module both finds an object and does something with it, let the caller find the object and pass it in, or let the module return a value that the caller uses.

- If a class has business logic tangled up with the mechanics of `method_missing`, use *Isolate Dynamic Receptor.*

What to Look for Next

◁ **Communication:** Splitting a module into smaller pieces will improve the way your code communicates your design: Be sure to choose meaningful names for the new modules and methods you create here. Look again at the old and new modules for any **Uncommunicative Name** that could now be simplified or cleaned up.

• **Simplicity:** If you created a new class, look at each method that references it for examples of **Feature Envy**: Fixing these will flesh out the new class and may expose some duplication among its new behaviors.

↯ **Testability:** Revisit the fixtures for this module's unit tests. You may be able to simplify them or split some tests so that they become simpler tests of the extracted code.

Exercises

Exercise 12.1: Feature Envy

Look back at Exercise 5.2. In `Report.report`, notice how the information being print-ed is obtained by looking "inside" the `Robot` and the `Machine`s.

A. Fix these two examples of **Feature Envy**.

B. What new smell(s) were introduced into this code by doing that?

C. Can you fix the new smell? If not, would you prefer to leave the code as it is now, or as it was to begin with? Explain your answer.

See page 239 for solution ideas.

Exercise 12.2: Walking a List

Consider the following partially developed code:

```
require 'agency'
require 'theater'
require 'test/unit'

class BookingTest < Test::Unit::TestCase
  def test_two_seats_anywhere
    adelphi = Theater.new('x-xxxx-xxxx')
    assert_equal([1,6], Agency.book(2, adelphi))
  end
end

class Theater
  attr_reader :seats

  def initialize(seats)
    @seats = seats.split(//)
  end
end

class Agency
  def self.book(num_reqd, theater)
    free_seats = []
    theater.seats.each_with_index do |item, index|
      free_seats << index if item == '-'
```

```
      end
      return nil if free_seats.empty?
      free_seats[0..num_reqd]
   end
end
```

A. In what way is `Agency` inappropriately intimate with `Theater`?

B. What is the simplest strategy for fixing this smell?

See page 239 for solution ideas.

Exercise 12.3: Middle Man

Consider this class:

```
require 'forwardable'

class SimpleQueue
  extend Forwardable

  def initialize
    @elements = []
  end

  def_delegator :@elements, :shift, :remove_front
  def_delegator :@elements, :push, :add_rear

  def_delegators :@elements, :clear, :first, :length
end

require 'test/unit'
require 'simple_queue'

class SimpleQueueTest < Test::Unit::TestCase
  def testQ
    q = SimpleQueue.new
    q.add_rear("E1")
    q.add_rear("E2")
    assert_equal "E1", q.remove_front
    assert_equal "E2", q.remove_front
    assert_equal 0, q.length
  end
end
```

A. Use *Remove Middle Man* so that the queue is no longer a middle man for the Array. Is this an improvement?

B. Put the middle man back in via *Hide Delegate*.

See page 240 for solution ideas.

Exercise 12.4: Cart (Challenging)

Consider these classes:

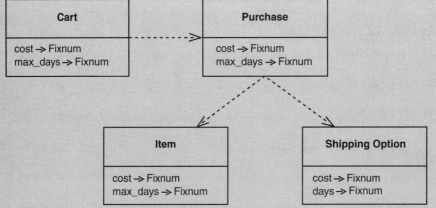

Here is `Cart.cost`:

```
class Cart
  def cost
    total = 0
    @purchases.each do |purch|
      total += purch.item.cost + purch.shipping.cost
    end
    return total
  end
end
```

A. Write the implied classes (and tests). (The `max_days` method computes the largest number of days for any ShippingOption in the purchase.)

B. Apply *Hide Delegate* so Cart accesses only Purchase directly.

C. *Hide Delegate* causes the middle man class (Purchase) to have a wider interface—that is, it exposes more methods. But applying that refactoring can open up a way to make the interface narrower. Explain this apparent contradiction.

D. Use this line of reasoning to narrow the Purchase interface.

E. Notice that the generic Integer class is used to represent money. If we want to change to a Money class, would it be easier to make the change before or after the delegation changes?

See page 240 for solution ideas.

Exercise 12.5: Utility Functions

A. Look again at the code sample in Exercise 5.1. `Matcher.match` is a **Utility Function** because it doesn't depend on the state of the Matcher instance. How would you fix this?

B. Look again at the code sample in Exercise 5.2. Is `Report.report` a **Utility Function**? If so, devise a strategy for fixing it.

See page 240 for solution ideas.

Exercise 12.6: Attributes

Perhaps the easiest way for an object to open itself up to **Inappropriate Intimacy (General Form)** is for it to define simple attribute methods via `attr`, `attr_reader`, `attr_writer`, or `attr_accessor`.

A. Some argue that every attribute accessor gives rise to the **Inappropriate Intimacy** smell. Do you agree? Justify your answer, giving counterexamples if you disagree.

B. By their very nature, Structs invite **Inappropriate Intimacy**. Indeed, it might be argued that every Struct is an **Open Secret**. Should Structs therefore be avoided?

See page 241 for solution ideas.

Exercise 12.7: Message Chains

The *Law of Demeter* states that a method shouldn't talk to strangers—that is, a method should only send messages to

- instance variables
- `self`
- its own arguments
- or the objects it creates

(See Andrew Hunt and David Thomas' *The Pragmatic Programmer* [17] for more details.)

Consider the following code fragments. Imagine they are each sitting in methods on some object:

- `@customers.map { |p| p.surname }.sort.uniq`
- `@report.machine[2].bin.contents` (based on Exercise 5.2)
- `@mock.should_receive(:sample).times(2).and_return(12, 19)` (based on FlexMock)

A. Which of them, if any, violate the Law of Demeter?

B. Which of them is an example of a **Message Chain**?

See page 241 for solution ideas.

CHAPTER 13

Accommodating Change

Some problems become most apparent when you try to change your code. (Most of the other smells we've discussed can be detected by looking at the code statically.)

Ideally, one changed decision affects one place in the code. When it doesn't work out that way, it's a sign of duplication in the code.

Addressing these smells has a side benefit: Many times it makes the code easier to test.

In this chapter we'll cover the following smells:

- **Divergent Change**, in which a class or module changes too frequently
- **Shotgun Surgery**, in which a simple change causes change everywhere
- **Parallel Inheritance Hierarchies**, in which changes to one hierarchy must mirror changes to another
- **Combinatorial Explosion**, in which a class hierarchy has too many dimensions

Divergent Change

What to Look For

• You find yourself changing the same module for different reasons.

(For contrast, see **Shotgun Surgery**, the next smell we discuss.)

Why This Is a Problem

↝ **Flexibility:** If a module needs to change for many different reasons, you may quickly find that two developers need to change it at the same time. So the module becomes a bottleneck, slowing down progress.

◎ **Abstraction:** Worse, a module with high "churn" may never stabilize, and so may never come to reliably represent a useful domain abstraction. In *Object-Oriented Software Construction* [23] Bertrand Meyer recommended that we should strive to be able to add functionality without modifying existing classes, because their stable, tested state represents an investment. (Recall that in Chapter 8, "Duplication," we talked about Parnas' dictum that a module should have only one secret.)

How It Got This Way

The module picks up more responsibilities as it evolves, with no one noticing that two different types of decision are involved.

What to Do

• It's likely that frequent change has introduced conditional logic; look through the module for **Simulated Polymorphism** and break up the code using the refactorings suggested there.

• If the module has too many (i.e., more than one) responsibilities, consider the refactorings we suggest for fixing a **Greedy Module**. Use *Extract Class* or *Extract Module* to separate the responsibilities.

• If several classes share the same decisions or variation points, you may be able to consolidate them into new classes (e.g., by *Extract Superclass* or *Extract Subclass*) or extract a common module to serve as a mix-in. In the limit, these extracted classes or modules can form a layer (e.g., a persistence layer).

What to Look for Next

◁ **Communication:** One way or another you've moved responsibilities out of this module. Review all of the modules you touched, looking for **Uncommunicative Names** and **Inconsistent Names** to make sure this new, cleaner design is expressed clearly.

↝ **Flexibility:** Your new design will likely be more robust to future changes. Review any new classes, modules, or methods you just created, looking particularly for **Feature Envy** and **Middle Man**, each of which may indicate your design still has a way to go before it can stabilize.

Shotgun Surgery

What to Look For

- Making a simple change requires you to change several classes or modules.

Why This Is a Problem

◁ **Communication:** You change a single decision and you have to change several classes, which probably means that the decision doesn't have a name, and consequently the application's design isn't being clearly communicated. That will cause current and future developers to need to search the code more, which may in turn lead to defects.

⤳ **Flexibility:** It probably also means that the decision hasn't been isolated from other decisions. So some modules may be harder to test than necessary, and some modules may churn for longer, perhaps never stabilizing.

How It Got This Way

One responsibility is split among several modules. There may be a missing class that would understand the whole responsibility, or perhaps an **Open Secret** has never been encapsulated. Or, this can happen through an overzealous attempt to eliminate **Divergent Change.**

What to Do

- Identify the class or module that should own the group of changes. It may be an existing module, or you may need to use *Extract Module* to create a new one. If it is an **Open Secret**, see the advice specific to that smell.

- Use *Move Field* and *Move Method* to put the functionality onto the chosen module. After the module not chosen is simple enough, you may be able to use *Inline Module* to eliminate it.

What to Look for Next

⋈ **Duplication:** If the new module embodies a pattern or a sequence of actions, you may find that several other modules had to compensate by implementing their own copies of those steps. Look for **Duplicated Code** where the new module could now be used instead.

◁ **Communication:** The missing decision is now represented by a module: Review its clients for **Feature Envy**, and review for **Inconsistent Names** among the methods it is acquiring.

↝ **Flexibility:** Fixing **Shotgun Surgery** will improve maintainability—because future changes of this same type will now be more localized. But by carving out this new module you may leave a hole behind; review all the modules you touched, looking for a **Middle Man**, **Dead Code**, or a **Lazy Class**.

Parallel Inheritance Hierarchies

What to Look For

- You make a new subclass in one hierarchy and find yourself required to create a related subclass in another hierarchy.

- You find two hierarchies where the subclasses have the same prefix. (The naming reflects the requirement to coordinate hierarchies.)

This is a special case of **Shotgun Surgery**, discussed earlier.

Why This Is a Problem

⋈ **Duplication:** Every time we need to change the hierarchy—for example, to add another case—we also have to change the other, parallel hierarchy.

◁ **Communication:** It's cumbersome and error prone, and probably doesn't communicate the intent of the design very well.

How It Got This Way

The hierarchies probably grew in parallel, a class and its pair being needed at the same time. As usual, it probably wasn't bad at first, but after two or more pairs get introduced, it becomes too complicated to change one thing. (Often both classes embody different aspects of the same decision.)

This smell may happen along the way while improving a particularly tangled situation.

What to Do

- Use *Move Field* and *Move Method* to redistribute the features in such a way that you can eliminate one of the hierarchies.

What to Look for Next

⋈ **Duplication:** As you merge classes from the two hierarchies, you may find **Duplicated Code** now coming together in the same place.

◁ **Communication:** Hopefully the merged classes now communicate the design more clearly; look carefully at the names now in use to make sure that is the case.

∇ **Size:** Having fewer classes means less code to understand. But each class in the merged hierarchy is now likely to be bigger than it was, so look out for **Large Module** and **Greedy Module**.

Combinatorial Explosion

What to Look For

- To introduce a single new concept, you must introduce multiple classes at various points of a class hierarchy.
- Each layer of a class hierarchy uses a common set of words (e.g., one level adds style information, and the next adds mutability).

Why This Is a Problem

⋈ **Duplication:** This is a relative of **Parallel Inheritance Hierarchies**, in which everything has been folded into one class hierarchy.

How It Got This Way

What should be independent decisions get implemented via a hierarchy.

What to Do

- If things aren't too far gone, you may be able to use *Replace Inheritance with Delegation*. (By keeping the same interface for the variants, you can create an example of the Decorator design pattern.)
- If the situation has grown too complex, you're in big-refactoring territory, and you can use *Tease Apart Inheritance*. (See Fields et al.'s *Refactoring, Ruby Edition* [11] for the details.)

What to Look for Next

⋈ **Duplication:** Fixing a **Combinatorial Explosion** is often a big shake-up for a lot of classes. As always, check the names you end up with, and check the code in the (old) hierarchy's clients for **Feature Envy** and related smells.

∇ **Size:** The classes of the (old) hierarchy are likely to be fewer and smaller now, because they deal with the design's complexities in a different way. Look through their clients for historical compromises such as **Nil Checks** or **Complicated Boolean Expressions**.

Exercises

Exercise 13.1: CSV Writer

Consider this code to write Comma-Separated Value (CSV) files.

```ruby
class CsvWriter

  def write(lines)
    lines.each { |line| write_line(line) }
  end

private

  def write_line(fields)
    if (fields.length == 0)
      puts
    else
      write_field(fields[0])
      1.upto(fields.length-1) do |i|
        print ","
        write_field(fields[i])
      end
      puts
    end
  end

  def write_field(field)
    case field
      when /,/ then write_quoted(field)
      when /"/ then write_quoted(field)
      else print(field)
    end
  end

  def write_quoted(field)
    print "\""
    print field.gsub(/\"/, "\"\"")
    print "\""
  end
end
```

```
require "csv_writer"
require "test/unit"

class CsvWriterTest < Test::Unit::TestCase

  def test_writer
    writer = CsvWriter.new
    lines = []
    lines << []
    lines << ["only one field"]
    lines << ["two", "fields"]
    lines << ["", "contents", "several words included"]
    lines << [",", "embedded , commas, included", "trailing,"]
    lines << ["\"", "embedded \" quotes", "multiple \"\" quotes\"\"\""]
    lines << ["mixed commas, and \"quotes\"\"", "simple field"]

    # Expected:
    # -- (empty line)
    # only one field
    20 # two, fields
    # ,contents,several words included
    # ",","embedded, commas, included","trailing,"
    # """","embedded "" quotes","multiple """""" quotes"""""""
    # "mixed commas, and ""quotes""","simple field"

    writer.write(lines)
  end
end
```

A. How is this code an example of **Divergent Change**? (What decisions does it embody?)

B. Modify this code to write to an IO object passed in as an argument.

C. Starting again from the original code, modify the functions to return a string value corresponding to what the functions would have written. (Feel free to rename your classes and methods to match their new responsibilities.)

D. Which version seems better, and why? Which is easier to test?

E. Compare this class with `CSV::Writer` from the Standard Library. Which is easier to use?

See page 241 for solution ideas.

Exercise 13.2: Shotgun Surgery

Find examples of **Shotgun Surgery** in code you have access to. Some frequent candidates:

- Configuration information
- Logging
- Persistence
- Places where it takes two calls on an object to get something common done, and this "two-step" is used in several places

Exercise 13.3: Hierarchies in Rails

The various generators in Rails initially ensure that every controller inherits from `ActionController::Base` and every model inherits from `ActiveRecord::Base`. This sounds like a parallel inheritance hierarchy; is it?

See page 243 for solution ideas.

Exercise 13.4: Documents

Consider this class hierarchy:

```
Document
  AsciiDocument
    ZippedAsciiDocument
    RawAsciiDocument
    BriefAsciiDocument
  HtmlDocument
    RawHtmlDocument
    ZippedHtmlDocument
  MarcDocument
    BriefMarcDocument
    FullMarcDocument
```

A. What's the impact of adding a new compression type that all document types will support?

B. Rearrange the hierarchy so it's based first on compression (or none), then brief/full, then document type. Is this an improvement?

C. Describe a different approach, using the Decorator pattern.

See page 243 for solution ideas.

CHAPTER 14

Libraries

Any Ruby application will use libraries—be it the core or standard libraries, or third-party gems downloaded from RubyForge or a similar repository.

Libraries sometimes put us in a dilemma: We want the library to be different, and yet we don't want to change it. Even when it's possible to change a library, that can carry risk because it could affect other clients, and it could mean we would have to redo our changes for future versions of the library.

Sometimes, library code is a bit smelly in order that client code doesn't have to be. Micah Martin points out that a library that is so factored it has lots of public classes and no smells can be harder to use; it's helpful if the library makes a narrow, easy-to-use interface available.

In this chapter we'll cover the following smells:

- **Incomplete Library Module**, in which a library has a vital feature missing
- **Reinvented Wheel**, in which you've written code that already exists elsewhere
- **Runaway Dependencies**, in which unexpected dependencies emerge when reuse is attempted

Incomplete Library Module

What to Look For

- You're using a library module, and there's a feature you wish were provided, but it's not.

- You see client code implementing a feature that could be in the library. (This can be visible as duplication in the client code.)

Why This Is a Problem

In a statically typed language such as Java, an incomplete library can be a big problem because we can't add methods to a class in a jar file. In Ruby, however, we can add methods to any class or module at any time. So the main issue here is in finding an appropriate way to manage the extension of the library.

◎ **Abstraction:** Extending the library by monkey-patching usually leads to other later problems such as **Greedy Module**.

⤳ **Flexibility:** Several projects might extend a library in incompatible ways, leading to subtle duplication and extra work if the library changes.

How It Got This Way

The author of the module didn't anticipate your need (or declined to support it due to other trade-offs).

What to Do

- Use *Introduce Local Extension*: In your own application code add the missing methods to the module. However, if those new methods don't naturally form part of the abstraction represented by the library, this refactoring will create a **Greedy Module**.

- Alternatively, consider creating an Adapter or Wrapper to contain your extensions.

- If the extension is large, or if it becomes popular, consider using *Extract Module* to create a reusable library extension for use in other applications.

- After you've reused this extension in a couple of projects, check whether the owner of the library would consider incorporating your extension.

What to Look for Next

⋈ **Duplication:** Look at the other clients of this library, in every project you can find. Look for similar or overlapping extensions—**Alternative Modules with**

Different Interfaces—and look for compromises that may have been made due to the missing features.

◁ **Communication:** Make sure the names you have chosen for the additional classes and methods fit well with the *System of Names* used by the original library. If the extended library now exhibits **Inconsistent Names**, you may have a clash of domain representations between the library and your application. Consider resolving this by wrapping the library in an Adapter, instead of extending it.

Simplicity: Look at the module you just extended: Is it now Large or Greedy? Perhaps this larger interface would be better designed by creating a Wrapper or Adapter for the library, using smaller classes.

Reinvented Wheel

What to Look For

- You've coded an algorithm with exactly the same behavior as an existing core Ruby or standard library feature.

Why This Is a Problem

⋈ **Duplication:** Your code duplicates existing code. This is a variant of **Alternative Modules with Different Interfaces** at the level of an algorithm or a few methods.

◁ **Communication:** Other developers have to waste time reading your code carefully to understand its effects.

• **Simplicity:** It is possible that there are defects in your code that aren't present in the library version of the same functionality.

When to Leave It

If the existing library has defects or other shortcomings, you may have no choice but to reinvent the wheel.

How It Got This Way

The code was written by someone not familiar with Ruby's libraries. Or the Ruby libraries have evolved since your code was written, and now your version is obsolete.

If the existing library's API is inconvenient for your application, consider adding a Wrapper layer to morph the interface into one you can use.

What to Do

Fix this smell in the same way you would fix **Alternative Modules with Different Interfaces** (See Chapter 8, "Duplication").

What to Look for Next

▽ **Size:** Now that you have folded your own algorithm back into the libraries, you may find that the class it came from is now a **Lazy Class**—or at least contains some **Dead Code**.

◁ **Communication:** The library may use a different *System of Names* than you had, so check for **Inconsistent Names** in the area you just changed.

Runaway Dependencies

What to Look for

- You want to reuse a single class or module, but you have to drag in the whole application or several gems you don't need or want.

Why This Is a Problem

⤳ **Flexibility:** The "requires" relationship in Ruby is transitive: If A requires B and B requires C, then A depends on C and needs it in order to load. This could cause code to be copied and edited, rather than reused as is.

How It Got This Way

It's usually easy to just instantiate objects where you need them. And that, in turn, means just adding `require` statements where you need them. And so the snowball begins.

What to Do

In general, *Dependency Inversion* is a large refactoring—one that can take several coding sessions to complete. Assuming there's just one class you want to reuse:

- Sometimes the offending `require` calls are not needed, perhaps being a hangover from earlier refactoring; this **Dead Code** can simply be deleted.

- If your code instantiates third-party objects, use *Parameterize Method* to push the call to `new` out toward the application's edges. Then delete the corresponding `require` call.

- If your class inherits from a third-party class, treat this as if it were a case of **Implementation Inheritance**.

What to Look for Next

⋈ **Duplication:** Gathering together the uses of a third-party module could reveal **Duplicated Code** or **Feature Envy** in its client classes.

Exercises

Exercise 14.1: Layers (Challenging)

One way to deal with libraries is to put them beneath a layer. This lets you isolate the bulk of your code from direct dependency on other libraries. Consider these two alternatives:

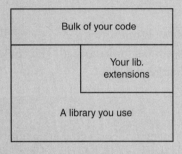
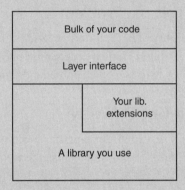

A. Redraw this as a UML package diagram showing dependencies.

B. Explain how the bulk of your code does or does not depend on the library code in each of these situations.

C. What effects does this layering have in terms of:

   • Conceptual integrity?
   • Portability?
   • Performance?
   • Testing?

D. What mechanisms do you have available to enforce the layering (that is, what stops someone from turning the second approach into the first one?)

See page 244 for solution ideas.

Exercise 14.2: Closed Classes (Challenging)

Some languages provide ways to "close" a class definition; in Java, for example, one cannot add methods to an existing class, and by making a class `final`, one can even prevent it from being subclassed. Ruby, however, allows you to add methods to an existing class or to change the definition of standard methods. Imagine this in your own application code:

```
class Array
  def length
    37
  end
end
```

This language feature gives the Ruby programmer great freedom and makes the *Introduce Local Extension* refactoring trivial.

A. What are the possible downsides of Ruby's open classes, both for library reuse and for application development?

B. Can you devise any means to discourage the abuse of Ruby's open classes?

C. Can you devise any means to create closed classes in Ruby?

See page 245 for solution ideas.

Exercise 14.3: A Missing Function

Consider the Zumbacker Z function, at the core of your application. (In fact, it's such a commonly used function in your domain that you're a little surprised it's not in the Ruby core libraries already.) It's defined:

```
Z(x) = abs(cos(x) + sin(x) - exp(x))
```

A. How could you handle the problem of Math being an incomplete library?

See page 245 for solution ideas.

PART III

Programs to Refactor

A Simple Game

This example involves refactoring and test-driven design.[1]

Suppose we've decided to develop an application to play games in the tic-tac-toe family: squares occupied by different markers. In tic-tac-toe you have a 3 × 3 grid, and you try to put your mark in three boxes in a row. In Connect Four by Hasbro you have a rectangular grid and try to get four boxes in a row, but columns have to be filled from bottom to top. We'll start with a simplified version of tic-tac-toe and work our way up to the general case.

Code

Here are some tests and the first version of the code:

```
require 'test/unit'
require 'tic_tac_toe'

class GameTest <Test::Unit::TestCase

  def test_default_move
    game = Game.new("XOX" +
                    "OX-" +
                    "OXO")

    assert_equal(5, game.move('X'))
    game = Game.new("XOX" +
                    "OXO" +
                    "OX-")
    assert_equal(8, game.move('O'))
```

---

1. The source code for this example is at http://github.com/kevinrutherford/rrwb-code.

```
      game = Game.new("---" +
                      "---" +
                      "---")
    assert_equal(0, game.move('X'))

      game = Game.new("XXX" +
                      "XXX" +
                      "XXX")
    assert_equal(-1, game.move('X'))
  end

  def test_find_winning_move
    game = Game.new("XO-" +
                    "XX-" +
                    "OOX")
    assert_equal(5, game.move('X'))
  end

  def test_win_conditions
    game = Game.new("---" +
                    "XXX" +
                    "---")
    assert_equal('X', game.winner())
  end
end

class Game
    attr_accessor :board

    def initialize(s, position=nil, player=nil)
      @board = s.dup
      @board[position] = player unless position == nil
    end

    def move(player)
      (0..8).each do |i|
        if board[i,1] == '-'
          game = play(i, player)
          return i if game.winner() == player
        end
      end

      (0..8).each { |i| return i if board[i,1] == '-' }
      return -1
    end
```

```
    def play(i, player)
      Game.new(board, i, player)
    end

    def winner
      if board[0,1] != '-' && board[0,1] == board[1,1] &&
          board[1,1] == board[2,1]
       return board[0,1]
      end

      if board[3,1] != '-' && board[3,1] == board[4,1] &&
          board[4,1] == board[5,1]
       return board[3,1]
      end

      if board[6,1] != '-' && board[6,1] == board[7,1] &&
          board[7,1] == board[8,1]
       return board[6,1]
      end

      return '-'
    end
end
```

Notice that the `winner` method is simplified: You win by getting three in a row horizontally. Notice also that the heuristics for what to play are primitive: Win if you can, play anything otherwise. We'll migrate toward something capable of more sophisticated strategies.

Refactoring

Exercise 15.1: Smells
Go through this code and identify smells.

See page 246 for solution ideas.

Exercise 15.2: Easy Changes
It's not always easy to know what to do with code. Let's fix some of the easy things first, one at a time.

- **Uncommunicative Name**: The method name `move` isn't descriptive enough. Change it to `best_move_for`.

- **Uncommunicative Name**: The variable `i` doesn't explain much either. Change it to `move`.
- **Open Secret**: The value –1 is a flag value; create a constant `NO_MOVE` to represent it.
- **Open Secret**: The string nature of the board is exposed, and the check for a board character being a '-' is really a check that the square is unoccupied. Extract a method to do this, and name it appropriately.

There's **Duplicated Code** in `best_move_for`, because we iterate over the squares on the board twice—once to find a winning move, and again to find a default move. One way to handle this would be to extract each pass into a method: As we add more strategies (we have two thus far), we could imagine each strategy getting its own method. An alternative would be to merge the two loops and handle things in one pass through the possible moves. We'll take the latter approach.

Exercise 15.3: Fuse Loops

Fuse Loops is a refactoring that combines two loops into one. It's a standard optimization used by compilers, but it's not in Fowler's or Fields' *Refactoring* catalog. (You need to be careful about applying this refactoring; it can reduce communication and encourage violations of the Single Responsibility Principle if applied to adjacent loops that are only coincidentally related.) As always, the refactoring should be done in small steps, maintaining safety at all times.

A. First, notice that both loops currently have side effects: We'll eliminate them by collecting all the **return** statements together at the end. For each loop introduce a temporary variable to cache the loop's result; be sure not to change it once it has a value.

B. Move the body of the second loop into the first, and delete the second loop entirely. (Remember to check that the tests still pass after each change.) If necessary, simplify the body of the loop so that the `can_play?` check occurs only once.

C. Put on a development hat for a moment: It's not necessary to stop when we find a viable move—that is, there's no harm in trying each possible move provided we prefer wins to defaults. So, you can delete any conditional code that prevents a cached value from being overwritten. Run the tests again and be sure you haven't changed anything important. You may have to change the tests. What does this tell you?

D. In general, when is it safe to merge two loops?

See page 246 for solution ideas.

Exercise 15.4: Result

Now we have a single loop, but the condition to decide what to return is still a little complicated. Your code probably looks something like ours:

```
return winning_move if winning_move != NO_MOVE
return default_move if default_move != NO_MOVE
return NO_MOVE
```

How would you simplify this?

See page 246 for solution ideas.

Exercise 15.5: Next

It's good practice to pause at regular intervals and review the new state of the code. What refactorings would you tackle next?

There are still a lot of magic numbers floating around. The `winner` method is full of them, for example. We'll tackle them in stages.

Exercise 15.6: Constants

The 8 in `best_move_for` is a **Derived Value**. Name some constants and rewrite the method.

See page 246 for solution ideas.

At this point, we're going to explore two different paths through the space of possible refactorings for the code. Make sure your current state is backed up—preferably in a version control system such as Subversion—because we'll be coming back to this point later.

Chapter 15: A Simple Game

Exercise 15.7: Checking for Wins

A. The conditionals in `winner` have **Duplicated Code**—each checks whether a particular row in the grid is filled with identical tokens. Fold these three checks together into a loop that iterates over the rows.

B. Now switch to a development hat. Currently we're not yet playing tic-tac-toe because we're only allowing horizontal three-in-a-row wins. Extend the `winner` method to allow vertical and diagonal wins. (Be sure to add some tests before you begin.)

C. Do you think the refactoring you did in step A (looping over the rows) made step B (adding more checks) easier or harder? What might you have done differently?

During the course of those last few steps we extracted a few helper methods such as `row`:

```
def row(index)
   [board[index*COLUMNS,1], board[index*COLUMNS+1,1],
    board[index*COLUMNS+2,1]]
end
```

It took a couple of tries to get the calculations correct, so let's fix that now.

Exercise 15.8: Representations

The game board is represented as a `String`, which may or may not be the most natural choice. It's certainly an **Open Secret**.

A. What other parts of your code currently depend on the choice of a `String` for the game board? Suggest refactorings you could perform to reduce the spread of that knowledge.

B. Suggest at least two other ways we might represent the game's state. Assess their pros and cons (without changing any code at this stage).

C. Define a method `cell(row, col)` that returns the token at the given location on the game board. Replace all direct reads of the string by calls to `cell`.

D. The only place where a token is actually placed on the board is in the constructor; and the constructor's conditional parameters are only fired by the `play` method. Rewrite `play` so that the constructor only takes a single parameter.

See page 246 for solution ideas.

Exercise 15.9: Refactoring Order

Now go back to your saved code and do Exercises 15.7 and 15.8 again—but this time do 15.8 first. Was one order harder than the other? Why is that?

We could pursue improving the representation a lot further—and when you have completed this chapter you may wish to do just that. But for now, we'll return to our vision of developing a general-purpose token-placing game.

Exercise 15.10: Winning Combinations

There's another hidden constant: the number in a row that it takes to win. (Recall that we mentioned Connect Four as one of the variations we eventually want to support.) Suppose we change to a 5 × 5 grid and want four in a row to win. How easy is that to put into the code?
(You needn't add this feature; this is more of a thought question.)

Most of the refactorings we've applied so far have been obvious improvements. Now it's time to grow and improve the program through a combination of refactoring and new implementation. But it's not clear what's best to do next.

You can think of this as *subjunctive programming*. The subjunctive tense is the one used to talk about possible worlds ("If I were a rich man..."). Our stance is that we'll try some ideas and see where they lead, but if they don't work out, that's okay.

Two things make subjunctive programming bearable: a partner, so you can kick around ideas, and a source control system, so you can back out anything you don't like.

The general direction is that we want to allow more sophisticated strategies than "win if you can and play arbitrarily otherwise." One possible direction here is to create a Move object and let it evaluate how good the move is.

Exercise 15.11: Iterator

In `best_move_for` we're running a loop over the integers representing possible moves, an **Open Secret**. Turn this into an iterator over the moves.

A. Extract an `each_move` method that yields the moves one by one to `best_move_for`.

B. Our new iterator delivers all moves, legal or not. Move the `can_play?` test into `each_move` so it only yields legal moves.

C. Introduce a `Move` struct that holds an integer move, and have `each_move` return instances of it.

Currently, we're just looping through possible moves, trying to select the best one, following a simple rule: Wins are best, anything else is acceptable. But wins are rare; we'd like to pick a good intermediate move, as some moves are better than others. We can think of each move as having a score: how good it is. Just to have something to work with, we'll say a win is worth 100 points and any other move is worth 0 points. (We could also think of wins by the opposing player being worth −100 points, but we won't check for those yet.)

Note that we're out of the domain of refactoring; we're making a semantic change to our program. That's the way development works. Because refactoring makes things cleaner, we can see better ways to do them.

Development Episodes

Exercise 15.12: Scores

Modify `best_move_for` to calculate scores for moves and return the move with the best score. (Hint: Instead of tracking the `winning_move` and `default_move`, keep track of `best_score` and `best_move`.)

Notice how a score is associated with a particular move. Perhaps it should be part of the `Move` object. Doing this might let us eliminate tracking of the integer score from the main loop.

Exercise 15.13: Comparing Moves

Move the score calculation:

A. In order to calculate the score, `Move` objects need to know the game and the player. Add those to `Move`.

B. Move the calculation of a move's score onto the `Move` object.

C. Now `best_move_for` is calculating the maximum of the scores of the playable moves, "by hand." But there's a method on `Enumerable` that does just that. Implement a comparison operator (`<=>`) for `Move`.

D. Replace `each_move` by a method that returns an array of the playable `Move`s, and replace the bulk of `best_move_for` by a call to `max`.

This is often how it goes. We refactored to create a method that yielded the moves, and then later we replaced that by a different approach. It doesn't mean our first try was bad; we just learned more as the overall shape of the code shifted and simplified.

The program calculates every possible move and response. This is feasible for tic-tac-toe, and perhaps also would be okay if we were to convert it to Hasbro's Connect Four, but certainly not feasible for a game like chess or Go. Eventually, we would have to develop a new strategy.

One way to handle this is to limit the depth to which we search. Suppose we establish a depth cutoff value; searches deeper than this will simply return "don't know." We will pass an additional parameter representing the current depth.

Exercise 15.14: Depth

Use *Add Parameter* to add a depth parameter, and maintain its value properly. After you have the depth parameter, add an early check that returns when things are too deep. What move will you return?

Exercise 15.15: Caching

We can think of performance tuning as *refactoring for performance:* It tries to keep the program performing the same job, only faster. If we think of the program as exploring the game tree of possible moves, we might see the same board via different paths. Could you cache the moves so you could recognize boards you've already rated?

Exercise 15.16: Balance

Do we have the right balance in our objects? Are there any missing objects? Which should calculate the score, Game or Move? Try shifting it around and see the consequences. Do some of these decisions make caching easier or harder?

Exercise 15.17: New Features

Add some new features, test-first; make sure to refactor along the way.

A. Score a win by the opponent at –100.

B. Extend to $m \times n$ tic-tac-toe.

C. Require that a move be at the lowest empty space in a column.

Exercise 15.18: Min-Max

A. Add another feature: Use the min-max algorithm, described in any Artificial Intelligence (AI) textbook. Instead of just saying, "non-wins are all the same," you say: "Choose my best move, assuming the opponent makes the move that's worst for me." The opponent uses the same rule. How is this reflected in the code? Is it a trick to use it?

B. There's an extension to that approach, called alpha-beta pruning. It says that we can avoid searching parts of the tree by establishing cutoff values. Find an AI book, and consider what it would take for you to implement such an approach. Is this a refactoring, new development, or what?

Exercise 15.19: Do-Over?

This has been an experiment in changing the structure of an application. There are other paths we could take. In particular, the balance between classes could go down a different path. The first tests assumed 3 × 3 tic-tac-toe; it would be interesting to start 1 × 1 and work to $m \times n$ that way, letting 3 × 3 be a special case.
   Would it be better to start over or work from the current base?

CHAPTER 16

Time Recording

Imagine your team or department uses a tool to track the hours spent on client projects so that your company can invoice correctly at the end of each month.[1] The tool is a Ruby script offering a simple command-line interface; it's used like this (the last argument is always a project name, and -u selects a user):

```
$ timelog -h 4.5 project1
$ timelog -u bill -h 6 project2
$ timelog --date 2008-08-26 -h 2 project1
$ timelog project2
jun-08  15.0
jul-08 128.5
aug-08 117.0
Total   260.5
$ timelog -u kevin project1
2008-06  15.0
2008-07  76.0
2008-08  17.5
Total    108.5
$
```

Here is the script itself:

```
#! /usr/bin/ruby
#
# Usage:
#
# timelog [--user USERNAME] [[--date d] [--hours] hrs] project
#
```

---

1. The source code for this example is at http://github.com/kevinrutherford/rrwb-code.

```ruby
require 'ostruct'
require 'optparse'
require 'optparse/date'

def parse_options(argv)
  options = OpenStruct.new
  OptionParser.new do |opts|
    opts.banner = "Usage: #{$0} [options] project_name"

    opts.on("-d", "--date DATE", Date,
        "Specify the date on which hours were worked") do |d|
      options.date = d
    end
    opts.on("-h", "--hours NUM", Float,
        "The number of hours worked") do |hrs|
      options.hours = hrs
    end
    opts.on("-u", "--user USERNAME", String,
        "Log time for a different user") do |user|
      options.user = user
    end
    opts.on_tail("-?", "--help", "Show this message") do
      puts opts
      exit
    end
  end.parse!

  if argv.length < 1
    puts "Usage: #{$0} [options] project_name"
    exit
  end

  if argv.length == 2
    hours = argv.shift
    options.hours = hours.to_f
  end

  if options.hours && options.hours <= 0.0
    raise OptionParser::InvalidArgument, hours
  end

  options.project = argv[0]
  options
end

TIMELOG_FOLDER = ENV['TL_DIR'] || '/var/log/timelog'
TIMELOG_FILE_NAME = 'timelog.txt'
TIMELOG_FILE = TIMELOG_FOLDER + '/' + TIMELOG_FILE_NAME
```

```ruby
def report(options)
  records = IO.readlines(TIMELOG_FILE)
  records = records.grep(/^#{options.project},/)
  records = records.grep(/,#{options.user},/) if options.user
  months = Hash.new(0.0)
  total = 0.0
  records.each do |record|
    project, user, date, hours = record.split(/,/)
    total += hours.to_f
    y, m, d = date.split(/-/)
    months["#{y}-#{m}"] += hours.to_f
  end
  lines = months.keys.sort.map { |month|
    "%-7s %8.1f" % [month, months[month]]
  }
  lines << "Total %8.1f" % total
  lines.join("\n")
end

def log(options)
  options.user ||= ENV['USERNAME']
  options.date ||= Date.today.to_s
  File.open TIMELOG_FILE, 'a+' do |f|
    f.puts "#{options.project}," "#{options.user}," +
    "#{options.date},#{options.hours}"
  end
end

if __FILE__ == $PROGRAM_NAME
  options = parse_options(ARGV)
  if options.hours.nil?
    puts report(options)
  else
    log(options)
  end
end
```

The script also has a few end-to-end tests:

```ruby
require 'test/unit'
load 'timelog.rb'

class TimelogTest < Test::Unit::TestCase
  def setup
  @varlog_size = File.size(TIMELOG_FILE) if
    File.exist?(TIMELOG_FILE)
    File.delete(TIMELOG_FILE_NAME) if
```

```
    File.exist?(TIMELOG_FILE_NAME)
  ENV['TL_DIR'] = '.'
  assert_equal('',
    'ruby timelog/timelog.rb -u fred -h 6 proj1')
  assert_equal('',
    'ruby timelog/timelog.rb -u jim -h 7 proj1')
  assert_equal('',
    'ruby timelog/timelog.rb -u alice -h 4.5 proj1')
end

def teardown
  if File.exist?(TIMELOG_FILE)
    assert_equal(@varlog_size, File.size(TIMELOG_FILE),
      "log file #{TIMELOG_FILE} should be unchanged")
  end
  File.delete(TIMELOG_FILE_NAME) if
    File.exist?(TIMELOG_FILE_NAME)
end

def test_project_total
  rpt = 'ruby timelog/timelog.rb proj1'.split("\n")[-1]
  assert_equal(17.5, rpt.split[1].to_f)
end

def test_project_total_for_missing_project
  rpt = 'ruby timelog/timelog.rb proj2'.split("\n")[-1]
  assert_equal(0, rpt.split[1].to_f)
end

def test_user_total
  rpt = 'ruby timelog/timelog.rb --user fred proj1'
  rpt = rpt.split("\n")[-1]
  assert_equal(6, rpt.split[1].to_f)
end

def test_user_total_for_missing_user
  rpt = 'ruby timelog/timelog.rb --user harry proj1'
  rpt = rpt.split("\n")[-1]
  assert_equal(0, rpt.split[1].to_f)
end

def test_user_total_for_missing_project
  rpt = 'ruby timelog/timelog.rb --user fred proj2'
  rpt = rpt.split("\n")[-1]
  assert_equal(0, rpt.split[1].to_f)
end
end
```

Notice that the script stores the record of project hours in a flat text file. This design helped to get the script developed and into use quickly, but it is now becoming a liability. For one thing, the script makes no attempt to prevent concurrent writes to the file. The company already has a MySQL database holding details of all staff and all projects, so it seems to make sense to store the time logs in there too. A meeting is held to decide whether to refactor the existing tool or write a replacement from scratch.

Exercise 16.1: Rewrite or Refactor?

Look at the tool's code. We need to replace it with a version that uses a different persistence mechanism, but which otherwise has the same features.

   A. What are the arguments for and against refactoring the existing script?

   B. Make a list of the script's code smells.

See page 247 for solution ideas.

The decision is made to refactor the existing code, replacing the flat file by a persistence layer sitting on the company's existing MySQL database. Your mission, should you choose to accept it, is to carry out that refactoring.

Preparing the Soil

It is a good idea to begin every project on a "green bar," so that you know you have working code as your starting point.

Exercise 16.2: Project Kick-Off

   A. Take whatever time you need to set up your development project for this exercise and run the tests.

   B. Take a moment to develop a strategy for this refactoring task; think about the steps you might need to take in order to accomplish it safely, without leaving anything broken.

One approach is to simply replace all of the file manipulation code with SQL queries. We think that's a bit risky, so instead we're going to try to break the problem into smaller pieces in order to avoid that kind of "big bang." Right now, all of the code is sitting in a small number of **Greedy Methods**. So the key to our success is in making some separation between the three parts of this application: presentation, domain, and persistence.

First, though, we need to make the refactoring process a little more safe.

Exercise 16.3: Test Coverage

A. Review the existing tests and identify areas where coverage is weak. (Concentrate on looking at the application as a "black box"; try not to be sidetracked by the code itself.)

B. Write the missing tests; for consistency, adopt the style and approach of the existing tests.

See page 248 for solution ideas.

Reviewing the tests, it becomes clear that many of them invoke the whole application just to test one method. Then there's that pesky global constant `TIMELOG_FILE`; it's already made testing sufficiently hard that the code uses an environment variable to get around it! We want to pass the file's path as a parameter, but there's currently nothing to pass it to.

Exercise 16.4: Application Object

A. Use *Extract Class* to create a new class representing the timelog application. Give the new class a constructor taking the file's name as a parameter.

B. Move the `report` and `log` methods over to the new class.

C. Refactor the tests to use those new methods. Is the environment variable needed now?

D. That last change lost us some test coverage. Is that a problem? What would you do about it?

The **Duplicated Code** in the tests is now some what more apparent; we have a lot of tests with this general form:

```
def test_project_total_for_missing_project
  rpt = @recorder.report('proj2', nil).split("\n")[-1]
  assert_equal(0, rpt.split[1].to_f)
end
```

That's a lot of code just to ask a project for its total hours!

Exercise 16.5: Testable Methods

Remove duplication in the tests by extracting more fine-grained and specific methods on the application object. (Hint: You will create half a dozen methods such as `total_hours_for(project)`.)

In the rest of this chapter, we are going to focus on changing the application's persistence mechanism, and hopefully we're going to do that without changing its command-line options (user input) or report formatting (output). However, the code currently makes that harder than necessary, because most of the application's behavior is still in **Greedy Methods** that deal with both persistence *and* formatting. In *Smalltalk Best Practice Patterns* [2], Kent Beck says, "Don't put two rates of change together." His approach to dealing with the resulting **Divergent Change** is to break the code into "lots of little pieces."

Exercise 16.6: Rates of Change

A. Look at the methods that contain code for reading or writing the file. Split each of these methods apart, so that report formatting is separated from file operations.

B. Use *Extract Class* on your application object to wrap the file methods together with the path to the file.

C. Refactor the application object's constructor so that its parameter is a whole `TimelogFile` instance by pushing the `TimelogFile`'s construction up into the tests and the top-level script. This deliberately introduces a little duplication; what are the mitigating factors in this case?

See page 248 for solution ideas.

As so often happens during a large refactoring such as this, the elimination of one smell can reveal another that was previously hidden. In the code for `timelog` right now, the recording and reporting methods communicate with the file methods using strings containing comma-separated values.

Exercise 16.7: Open Secrets

Fix these **Open Secret**s by introducing a new class to wrap the CSV strings. Look for opportunities to move code onto the new class. Can you use the new class to simplify any of the tests?

In the language of Cockburn's *Hexagonal Architecture* [9], the `TimelogFile` class you just extracted is an Adapter for the file. Ideally it will be very thin: It should know nothing about the application, and yet its interface (the set of public method signatures) should reveal nothing of the underlying technology. This interface is the variation point we will exploit as we switch to a SQL solution.

Exercise 16.8: Hexagonal Architecture (Challenging)

Draw a UML static model showing your current code in *hexagonal architecture* form [9]. Ensure that your model clearly identifies

- The dependencies between the classes (`<<using>>` relationships)

- The test class(es)

- The variation point

- The "middle hexagon" and the adapters

See page 248 for solution ideas.

It's starting to feel like we have the application a little more under control now. Admittedly, many more code smells remain, but we want our next series of steps to be informed by the problem at hand. It's time to look at the database.

Substitute Algorithm

Figure 16.1 shows a rough outline of the relevant parts of the existing corporate database.

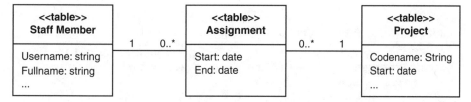

Figure 16.1 Existing Corporate Projects Database

Exercise 16.9: Data Smells

Refactoring mostly deals with code smells. But there are data smells too; the database community has notions of what constitutes a good data design.

A. What potential problems do you see in this database structure?

B. What changes to the database might address them? (Don't make the changes yet.)

See page 248 for solution ideas.

We'll bear these data smells in mind as we proceed, because one or two of them could impede our progress. But that's for the future; right now we need to sketch out a new design.

Exercise 16.10: Extending the Database

Design an extension to this schema to hold time records equivalent to those currently stored in the file. Try to do it so that the existing tables don't need to change.

See page 249 for solution ideas.

When we switch the code from file I/O to SQL, we want to do so in the presence of tests. We have a clear choice between two different approaches at this point: We could continue with the tests we have, or we could write some unit tests at the level of the variation point. We'll do the latter.

Exercise 16.11: Adapter Tests (Challenging)

A. Create a new test suite (call it `TimelogFileTests` or something similar) by copying the existing tests. You should now have twice as many passing tests!

B. For each test in the new suite, rewrite it so that it only uses `TimelogFile` and `Posting`. For example, instead of checking for the correct total hours, a rewritten test would check that the right `Posting` objects came back from the `TimelogFile`.

C. Now also rewrite the test setup so that it only uses `TimelogFile` and `Posting`.

D. Review your new test suite. You may find that some tests are now identical, in which case the duplicates can be deleted. Feel free to add extra tests for any edge cases you can now see.

It now appears that we have a layer of abstraction that completely hides the application's persistence mechanism. How confident are you that this is indeed true? After all, the `TimelogFile` adapter currently has only one use, and the application has only ever been run with one persistence adapter. The cold truth is that we can never be certain; at this point, we are completely reliant on the separation of responsibilities we made at Exercise 16.6. It's time now to put that design to the test.

We're going to make a new adapter for the SQL database, by copying the `Timelog-File` adapter and then gradually modifying it. This is a big, risky refactoring, so we'll take it in small steps.

Exercise 16.12: Database Technology

Our first task is to decide what Ruby gem(s) to use to access the SQL database.

Make a list of gems that might be suitable for the job. Pick one that suits your needs. If you haven't done so already, install your chosen gem.

See page 249 for solution ideas.

We'll now proceed with exercises based on the technology choice we just made. (If you chose differently, feel free to follow along with your chosen tool.)

Exercise 16.13: Database Tests (Challenging)

A. Copy the `TimelogFile` class and its tests to create new classes with "SQL" or "Database" in their names. Switch the new tests over to calling the new adapter. You should now have three suites of passing tests!

B. Augment the new test setup so that it also creates an equivalent fixture in a database. Drop, create, and populate all of the tables in the setup (so that each test starts with a new set of tables), and use raw SQL to populate them with the same data that goes into the file. (Your setup should continue to populate the file too, so the current tests—which use the file adapter—should still pass.)

C. Add a parameter to the SQL adapter's constructor and pass in the information required for connecting to the test database. Ensure that every method in the new adapter has access to a database connection (even though the code still uses the file). (Hint: We used MySQL, so we passed a new object containing the hostname, username, password, and database name; this new object also got a method that would connect to the specified database.)

We can't think of any more safety harnesses—it's time now to code up the new adapter.

Exercise 16.14: Database Adapter (Challenging)

For each method in the new `SQLAdapter` class:

A. Use a database tool to work out the precise SQL query needed by the method. You may find at this point that you need to fix some of the schema smells identified in Exercise 16.9 earlier; if so, modify the test setup accordingly.

B. Use *Substitute Algorithm* to replace the existing code with the SQL query.

C. Run the tests after each change.

We're almost done. We have two persistence adapters, each with a set of unit tests. But right now we have only one set of integration tests.

Exercise 16.15: Integration Tests

Write a suite of tests to prove that the application works with the test database. Did you get any surprises? If so, could you have prevented them by doing anything differently earlier in this chapter?

Now it's time to make the final leap and switch the application to use the real live corporate database.

Exercise 16.16: Going Live

A. We are about to switch the script so that it uses the corporate database instead of the file. What are the risks involved in doing this? Can you think of any ways to mitigate them?

B. (Optional) Create a new database and populate it with fake "corporate" data. In your top-level script, create an instance of your database adapter, constructed to point at the real live corporate database. Pass that object to your application object's constructor. Perform whatever safety checks you think are necessary.

Optional Extras

There are many ways to design persistence to a relational database. One of the most popular uses the Active Record pattern (see Fowler's *Patterns of Enterprise Application Architecture* [12]). Indeed, if you have done any Rails development, you will already have used the `ActiveRecord` gem.

Exercise 16.17: Active Record (Challenging)

As an optional exercise, if you're feeling adventurous, refactor your current design to use the `ActiveRecord` gem instead of relying directly on a SQL API. Is it possible to follow the step-by-step approach we used earlier? What changes are required to the *variation point* interface in order to work with `ActiveRecord`?

The code for this chapter was not originally written test-first.

Exercise 16.18: Test-Driven Development (Challenging)

A. Reimplement this application from scratch, test-first; provide both flat file and SQL versions. Don't look at the old version while you develop the new one. What do you see?

B. The experiences of people who do test-driven development indicate that a different design often emerges than the one they expected. Did that happen for you? Is the code better? Are the tests better? How much did the original design influence you?

C. Assuming your test-driven code is different from the code you were working with before, would it be feasible to refactor the old code until it matches the new code? Are there refactorings not "in the book" that you need to transform your code? What code smells could guide you so that you would naturally refactor in that direction? Does this teach you anything about refactoring, or about test-driven development?

## CHAPTER 17

Calculator

In this chapter we'll look at a small calculator.[1] This one has two twists. One is that it's based on a stack like an old HP calculator. The second is that it knows units.

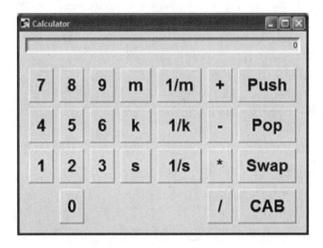

The stack approach lets us avoid dealing with the challenges of parsing (and tricky things like parentheses). It works like this: You can push values, and an operator such as + pops the top two items off the stack and replaces them with the sum. For example, 3 + 4 * 5 would be done with "3 PUSH 4 PUSH 5*+" whereas 3 * 4 + 5 would be "3 PUSH 4 * PUSH 5 +" and (3 + 4)/ * 5 would be "3 PUSH 4 + PUSH 5 *".

---

1. The source code for this example is at http://github.com/kevinrutherford/rrwb-code.

Units let us manipulate values with meters, kilograms, and seconds. Suppose we have something traveling 50 meters per second for 7 seconds. If we take $50\,m/s * 7\,s$, we get $350\,m$. (It would be entered "50 *m* 1/s PUSH 7s *".)

Code

It's easiest to understand these classes from the bottom up. First, we'll look at how units are managed with the class Dimension. Dimensions represent the MKS (meter/kilogram/second) values as a hash from the unit name to the exponent. (So m^2 is represented as {'m'=>2}.) Observe how multiplication, negation (inversion), and division manipulate the exponents.

```
class Dimension
  attr_reader :dimensions

  def initialize unit2int={}
    @dimensions = new_hash(unit2int)
  end

  def clone
    Dimension.new(new_hash(@dimensions))
  end

  def ==(other)
    return dimensions == other.dimensions
  end

  def *(other)
     new_dimensions = new_hash(dimensions)
     other.dimensions.each_pair {
       |key, value|
       sum = dimensions[key] + value
       new_dimensions[key] = sum
       new_dimensions.delete(key) if sum == 0
     }
     Dimension.new new_dimensions
  end
```

```ruby
  def -@
    new_dimensions = new_hash(dimensions)
    dimensions.each_pair{
      |key, value|
      new_dimensions[key] = -value
    }
    Dimension.new new_dimensions
  end

  def /(other)
    self * -other
  end

  def to_s
    return "" if dimensions.size == 0

    positives = ""
    negatives = ""
    dimensions.each{|key, value|
      positives += '*' + format(key, value) if value > 0
      negatives += '*' + format(key, -value) if value < 0
    }

    if (positives.length == 0)
      positives = "1"
    else
      positives = positives[1..-1]
    end

      if (negatives.length > 0)
        negatives = negatives[1..-1]
      end

      return positives if (negatives.length == 0)
      return positives + "/" + negatives
  end

  def format key, value
    return key if value == 1
    return key + "^" + value.to_s
  end

  private
  def new_hash initial_value
    result = Hash.new{|hash, key| hash[key] = 0 }
    result.merge!(initial_value)
    result
  end
end
```

Values are a pair, representing the product of an integer and a dimension. They support the various arithmetic operators, along with an operator that can extend either part of the pair. (For example, 327 extended with 8 becomes 3278, while *m* extended with 1/*s* becomes *m*/*s*.)

```ruby
require 'dimension'

class Value
  attr_reader :number, :dimension

  def initialize number, dimension
    @number = number
    @dimension = dimension
  end

  def clone
    Value.new(@number, @dimension.clone)
  end

  def extend v
    return Value.new(number * 10 + v, dimension) if
        v.kind_of? Integer
    return Value.new(number, dimension * v)
  end

  def +(other)
    raise "can't mix apples and oranges" if
        dimension != other.dimension
    Value.new(number + other.number, dimension)
  end

  def -(other)
    raise "can't mix apples and oranges" if
        dimension != other.dimension
    Value.new(number - other.number, dimension)
  end

  def *(other)
    Value.new(number * other.number,
        dimension * other.dimension)
  end

  def /(other)
    Value.new(number / other.number,
        dimension / other.dimension)
  end
```

```ruby
  def ==(other)
    (number == other.number) and (dimension == other.dimension)
  end

  def dimension
    @dimension
  end

  def to_s
    suffix = @dimension.to_s
    return @number.to_s if suffix.size == 0
    @number.to_s + '*' + @dimension.to_s
  end

end
```

Now look at Calculator, the core class. It holds the stack, and it knows whether the last value was pushed or calculated so it can know whether to extend a value or replace it.

```ruby
require 'value'

class Calculator
  attr_accessor :is_calculated

  def initialize start
    @default = start #Value.new 0, Dimension.new
    @stack = []
    @is_calculated = true
  end

  def default
    @default.clone
  end

  def top
    return default if @stack.size < 1
    @stack[-1]
  end

  def push value
    @is_calculated = false
    @stack.push value
  end

  def extend value
    start = @is_calculated ? default : top
    pop
```

```
    push start.extend(value)
end

def pop
  @is_calculated = true
  @stack.pop
end

def plus
  v2 = @stack.pop
  v1 = @stack.pop
  begin
      result = v1 + v2
  rescue
      result = default
  end

  @stack.push(result)
  @is_calculated = true
  self
end

def minus
  v2 = @stack.pop
  v1 = @stack.pop
  begin
      result = v1 - v2
  rescue
      result = default
  end

  @stack.push(result)
  @is_calculated = true
  self
end

def times
  v2 = @stack.pop
  v1 = @stack.pop
  begin
      result = v1 * v2
  rescue
      result = default
  end

  @stack.push(result)
  @is_calculated = true
```

```
    self
  end

def divide
  v2 = @stack.pop
  v1 = @stack.pop
  begin
      result = v1 / v2
  rescue
      result = default
  end

  @stack.push(result)
  @is_calculated = true
  self
  end

def binary_op_old op
  v2 = @stack.pop
  v1 = @stack.pop
  begin
      result = op.call(v1,v2)
  rescue
      result = default
  end

  @stack.push(result)
  @is_calculated = true
  self
end

def swap
  a = top
  pop
  b = top
  pop

  push a
  push b

  @is_calculated = true
end

  def to_s
    top.to_s
  end
end
```

Now we're moving up to the user interface. The `Calc_Controller` class coordinates
access to the calculator (and gives us a chance to test below the level of UI objects).

```ruby
require 'calculator'
require 'value'
require 'dimension'

  class Calc_Controller

  def initialize calculator
    @calculator = calculator
    @calculated = false
  end

  def digit n
    @calculator.extend(n)
  end

  def unit arg
    if @calculator.is_calculated
      @calculator.pop
      @calculator.push(Value.new(0, arg))
    else
      value = @calculator.top
      @calculator.pop
      value *= (Value.new 1, arg)
      @calculator.push value
    end

    @calculator.is_calculated = false
  end

  def push
    @calculator.push(Value.new(0, Dimension.new))
    @calculator.is_calculated = false
  end

  def pop
    @calculator.pop
  end

  def cab
    a = @calculator.top
    @calculator.pop
    b = @calculator.top
    @calculator.pop
    c = @calculator.top
    @calculator.pop
```

```
    @calculator.push b
    @calculator.push a
    @calculator.push c

    @calculator.is_calculated = true
  end

  def swap
    @calculator.swap
  end

  def plus
    @calculator.plus
  end

  def subtract
    @calculator.minus
  end

  def times
    @calculator.times
  end

  def divide
    @calculator.divide
  end

  def plus_old
    @calculator.binary_op(lambda{|a,b| a+b})
  end

  def to_s
    @calculator.to_s
  end

end
```

Finally, we get to the user interface proper, built on Tk. It delegates most of its work to the controller.

```
require 'tk'
require 'value'
require 'calculator'
require 'calc_controller'

@my_font = TkFont.new('helvetica 20 bold')
@calculator = Calculator.new(Value.new 0, Dimension.new)
```

```
@controller = Calc_Controller.new @calculator

def push
  @controller.push
  @my_text.value = @controller
end

def pop
  @controller.pop
  @my_text.value = @controller
end

def cab
  @controller.cab
  @my_text.value = @controller
end

def swap
  @controller.swap
  @my_text.value = @controller
end

def plus
  @controller.plus
  @my_text.value = @controller
end

def minus
  @controller.subtract
  @my_text.value = @controller
end

def times
  @controller.times
  @my_text.value = @controller
end

def divide
  @controller.divide
  @my_text.value = @controller
end

def extend_unit arg
  @controller.unit(arg)
  @my_text.value = @controller
end
```

```ruby
def extend_number n
  @controller.digit(n)
  @my_text.value = @controller
end

def plus_old
  @calculator.binary_op(lambda{|a,b| a+b})
  @my_text.value = @calculator
end

def make_button frame, name, p
  TkButton.new(frame, :text=>name,
      :font=>@my_font, :command =>p)
end

def make_digit root, number
  make_button(root, number, proc{extend_number number})
end

def make_unit root, unit
  make_button(root, unit, proc{extend_unit unit})
end

root = TkRoot.new { title "Calculator" }

output_frame = TkFrame.new(root).pack(
  'side'=>'top',
  'padx'=>10,
  'pady'=>10,
  'fill'=>'both')

button_frame = TkFrame.new(root).pack(
  'side'=>'bottom',
  'padx'=>10,
  'pady'=>10)

  @my_text = TkVariable.new

@calculated_result = TkEntry.new(output_frame) {
      width 75
      font @my_font
      state 'readonly'
      justify 'right'
      border 5
    }.pack(
      'fill'=>'y',
      'expand'=>'true')
```

```ruby
@calculated_result.textvariable = @my_text
@my_text.value = @calculator

b0 = make_digit(button_frame, 0)
b1 = make_digit(button_frame, 1)
b2 = make_digit(button_frame, 2)
b3 = make_digit(button_frame, 3)
b4 = make_digit(button_frame, 4)
b5 = make_digit(button_frame, 5)
b6 = make_digit(button_frame, 6)
b7 = make_digit(button_frame, 7)
b8 = make_digit(button_frame, 8)
b9 = make_digit(button_frame, 9)

bm = make_unit(button_frame, Dimension.new({'m'=>1}))
b1m = make_unit(button_frame, Dimension.new({'m'=>-1}))
bk = make_unit(button_frame, Dimension.new({'k'=>1}))
b1k = make_unit(button_frame, Dimension.new({'k'=>-1}))
bs = make_unit(button_frame, Dimension.new({'s'=>1}))
b1s = make_unit(button_frame, Dimension.new({'s'=>-1}))

b_plus = make_button(button_frame, '+', proc{plus})
b_minus = make_button(button_frame, '-', proc{minus})
b_times = make_button(button_frame, '*', proc{times})
b_divide = make_button(button_frame, '/', proc{divide})

b_push = make_button(button_frame, 'Push', proc{push})
b_pop = make_button(button_frame, 'Pop', proc{pop})
b_swap = make_button(button_frame, 'Swap', proc{swap})
b_cab = make_button(button_frame, 'CAB', proc{cab})

spaceholder = TkLabel.new(button_frame)

buttons = [
b7, b8, b9, bm, b1m, b_plus, b_push,
b4, b5, b6, bk, b1k, b_minus, b_pop,
b1, b2, b3, bs, b1s, b_times, b_swap,
spaceholder, b0, spaceholder, spaceholder,
    spaceholder, b_divide, b_cab]

items_per_row = 7

buttons.each_index { |i|
  buttons[i].grid(
    'column'=>(i%items_per_row),
    'row'=>(i/items_per_row),
    'sticky'=>'news',
```

```
    'padx'=>5,
    'pady'=>5)
}

Tk.mainloop
```

Refactoring

Here are some of the smells we noticed:

- **Uncommunicative Name:** `Calc_Controller` and `Calc_Screen` aren't standard Ruby class names (which wouldn't have underscores).
- **Duplicated Code:** Duplication between digits and units.
- **Duplicated Code:** Duplication across classes: `Calc_Screen`, `Calc_Controller`, and `Calculator` all have methods for the various operators.
- **Duplicated Code:** The button_frame is being passed many times, and it's the only value the parameter using it ever uses.
- **Dead Code:** There is an uncalled method `binary_pop_old()` in `Calculator`, and `plus_old()` in the main class.
- **Middle Man:** The arithmetic routines in `Calc_Controller` are pass-through methods to `Calculator`; it's not clear that the controller is pulling its weight.
- **Greedy Module:** Some stack methods are in the controller, some in the `Calculator`.
- **Inappropriate Intimacy (General Form):** There's redundant state in the controller and the calculator, trying to manage what happens when a value has been typed in and is due to be extended versus one that is calculated and should just be replaced.
- **Simulated Polymorphism:** The `extend()` method checks types to decide how to operate.
- **Feature Envy:** The `cab()` method does all its work with the calculator, so the work could be moved over there.
- **Duplicated Code:** All the calculation routines are very similar.
- **Suspicious Code:** The `Calculator` class hard-codes the default value, and the operators assume +-*/ are defined. (Values needn't be tied to the stack nature.)
- **Suspicious Code:** It seems suspicious that operators put in a default value (0) when anything suspicious happens ("5 m PUSH 2 s +" yields 0.) The value class definitely detects trying to add or subtract things with differing dimensions.
- **Long Method:** `Dimension`'s `*()` method seems longish; `to_s()` is definitely too long.
- **Duplicated Code:** The way positives and negatives are added is very similar.
- **Greedy Module:** Value knows its formatting.

- **Duplicated Code**: There's lots of similarity in the way the screen is set up (e.g., the calls `make_digit()` and `make_unit()`).

Where to begin? There's an art to it (especially with so many choices). We're reasonably confident that Value and Dimension stand on their own. We want to start at Calculator, as it's the heart of the system.

There are three things we want to accomplish first:

- Remove the direct dependency on the Value class and the default value. (What if we want to operate on integers instead of values? What would change?)
- Pull `cab()` over to the Calculator class.
- Eliminate the duplication in the operators.

Exercise 17.2: Clean up Calculator
Fix those problems in the Calculator class.

When we did this, we made all the arithmetic operators call a common `binary_op` method something like this:

```
def plus
  binary_op(lambda{|a,b| a+b})
end
```

Exercise 17.3: Straighten out `is_calculated`
It looks like `Calc_Controller` and `Calculator` are fighting over who owns the state that tracks whether a value is calculated. This is used so we know whether 58 extended by 3 should be 583 (if it's in the process of being entered) or just toss the 58 and put 3 on the stack (if the value on top of the stack was calculated). Figure out which class should own the state, and get this out of the other's hands.

(There are arguments for either class owning it, but not both.)

Exercise 17.4: Controller
The controller has two responsibilities: passing through to the calculator options and handling extension of the digits or the units. Harmonize and unify the two extension methods.

Did you notice the `extend()` method on Value? It's already prepared to work with either integers or Dimensions. (It does its work by type-checking. Can you think of a better approach?)

Exercise 17.5: Generic Calculator

Move the concrete binary operations over to the controller, so the `Calculator` class has no dependency on the specific operations, but only knows how to handle the generic binary case (where the particular operator is passed in). Move the `extend()` method over to the controller as well. At this point, Calculator has no dependency on the particular type. (For a bonus, try making it work with integers rather than Values. What other impacts are there?)

Exercise 17.6: UI Class

There are several places of duplication in `Calc_Screen`. Make it so `button_frame` is not passed around, since no other frame ever gets a button. Find a way to eliminate the duplication in all the controller calls. (Is this overkill?)

Exercise 17.7: Value and Dimension

The worst offense here is the formatting method. It's moderately big, and a bit hard to understand. More importantly, it ties formatting concerns into a domain-level object. (What if we were writing to a widget that could handle real superscripts and subscripts? This would just be in the way.)

Exercise 17.8: What Else?

What else can you do? It's often the case that applying the obvious refactorings reveals other more subtle opportunities.

Thank You

We hope that this and the other exercises have helped give you good practice at identifying code smells and applying refactorings that clean them up. We encourage you to participate in the community and keep learning. Good luck.

—Kevin and Bill

PART IV

Appendices

Answers to Selected Questions

We've included answers to some of the problems here. Where we've omitted answers, it's usually because we've asked you to work in your own code or because we want you to consider an issue on your own.

The Refactoring Cycle

Exercise 2.1: Simple Design

A. (a) Passes all tests. "If it doesn't have to work, I can give it to you right now."

   (b) Communicates. This makes an appeal to our intuition about future readers of our code (including ourselves).

   (c) No duplication. Duplicate code is asking for trouble; it's too vulnerable to changes in one place but not the other.

   (d) Fewest classes and methods. All things being equal, we prefer smaller code.

B. The bottom line is that there's an appeal to the reader's ability to understand; we'll tolerate duplication to achieve better understanding.

   Test code will sometimes have duplication, for communication reasons. For example, it may be easier to repeat an expected value rather than assign it to a variable and use the variable. That way, when you read the code, you know exactly what it was looking for, and you don't have to review code to find the variable and make sure nothing else changed it along the way.

Refactoring Step by Step

Exercise 3.1: Small Steps

Most refactorings reflect this attitude (safety even in mid-refactoring). You can some-times take a shortcut and bunch together a series of very similar steps—for example, when you have to change all of the callers during *Remove Parameter.*

Exercise 3.2: Inverse Refactorings

A. *Collapse Hierarchy* is inverted by *Extract Subclass.*

B. *Extract Method* is inverted by *Inline Method.*

C. *Hide Delegate* is inverted by *Remove Middle Man.*

D. *Inline Temp* is inverted by *Introduce Explaining Variable.*

E. *Parameterize Method* is inverted by *Replace Parameter with Explicit Methods.*

F. *Rename Method* is inverted by *Rename Method.*

Refactoring Practice

Exercise 4.1: Get to Know the Refactorings

A. The full cross-reference list will be large and somewhat subjective—we've omitted it for the sake of brevity.

B. Our impression is that *Move Method, Extract Class, Move Field,* and *Extract Method* are involved in fixing the most smells.

C. Quite a few refactorings aren't mentioned by any of the smells. Some are code ma-nipulation, where the refactoring provides a safe way to move between two valid alternatives. Others are a bit specialized (especially the "big" refactorings). Others are used as steps in applying another refactoring; the smell for the other refactor-ing triggers this one.

D. Everybody's list will be different. We considered these additional smells:

Intertwined Model and UI: *Duplicate Observed Data, Separate Domain from Presentation*

Unclear Communication: *Remove Assignment to Parameter, Replace Error Code with Exception, Replace Exception with Test, Replace Magic Number with Symbolic Constant, Split Temporary Variable*

Conditional Logic: *Consolidate Conditional Expression, Consolidate Duplicate Conditional Expression, Introduce Null Object, Replace Error Code with Exception, Replace Exception with Test, Replace Nested Conditional with Guard Clause, Replace Conditional with Polymorphism*

Measurable Smells

Exercise 5.1: Comments

A. One approach might be something along the lines of this:

```
class Matcher
  def clip(array, limit)
    array.map { |val| [val, limit].min }
  end

  def similar_values?(actual, expected, delta)
    ! actual.zip(expected).detect { |m| (m[0] - m[1]).abs > delta }
  end

  def match(expected, actual, clip_limit, delta)
    actual = clip(actual, clip_limit)
    actual.length == expected.length and
      similar_values?(actual, expected, delta)
  end
end
```

But there are other smells in this code; see Exercise 12.5 if you went further with your refactoring.

B. Code can usually communicate the *how* of something fairly well; it's not always able to communicate the *why* and it's almost impossible to communicate the *why not*.

When code becomes published for others to use, it is often important to include `rdoc` comments to document the API.

Exercise 5.2: Long Method

A. We identified the following blocks:

- Printing the header (line 3)
- Printing the state of the machines (lines 4–9)
- Printing the state of the robot (lines 10–15)
- Printing the footer (line 16)

B. You'll have something like this:

```
def Report.report(out, machines, robot)
  reportHeader(out)
  reportMachines(out, machines)
  reportRobot(out, robot)
  reportFooter(out)
end
```

We wouldn't stop here, but this would be a good first step. (We could either move toward a `Report` class or toward putting report methods on the `Machine` and `Robot` classes.)

C. It does make sense to extract a one-line method if it communicates better.

Exercise 5.3: Large Class

A. As with any useful class, some of String's methods are inherited from Object, whereas others are mixed in from the Enumerable and Comparable modules.

But in a pure object-oriented language such as Ruby, there's another way in which classes acquire methods: by fixing the **Feature Envy** and **Utility Function** smells. For example, in a procedural language, `to_i` might be a library function taking a single String parameter; here, it is moved onto the parameter's class—String in this case. And because there's only one kind of string in Ruby, the String class has acquired methods from all of the contexts in which it is used by the other core and standard library classes.

B. A String object is both a sequence of bytes and a piece of meaningful text. In addition to the mix-in methods, we found the following groups of methods in class String (yours may well vary):

String as a first-class object: `inspect`, `to_s`, etc.
String as a sequence of bytes: `[]`, `==`, `reverse`, etc.
String as a data container: `crypt`, `unpack`, etc.
Text formatting: `center`, `ljust`, `strip`, etc.
Text processing: `capitalize`, `downcase`, `tr`, etc.
Pattern matching: `index`, `split`, `sub`, etc.
String as a value: `next`, `to_i`, `upto`, etc.
String as a symbol name: `intern`, `to_sym`, etc.

C. On the one hand, aliases increase the size of the class's API, which can make it seem more daunting to search and understand. On the other hand, aliases improve the language's expressiveness and readability, and at the same time they lower the entry barrier for programmers coming to Ruby from other environments.

D. Strictly speaking, the non-! version of the method is redundant—for example, we could create a reversed copy of a String using

```
reversed_copy = String.new(original).reverse!
```

However, this is such a common operation that a method has been provided in order to avoid duplication.

Note also that the non-! version is "safe"—it doesn't modify its receiver. So by using a naming convention that makes it somewhat more natural to call the safe version of the method, Ruby helps us avoid the introduction of insidious defects.

E. On balance, we don't consider the size of the String API to be a smell. It's a special case: String lies at the heart of Ruby's power and expressiveness, and that's a tradeoff we're happy to make.

It might be argued that String could be subclassed, so that methods for specific purposes were only made available after conversion to a different object (pack and unpack are obvious candidates here). But for most uses, Ruby's efficacy as a scripting language would be compromised by breaking up String.

As a final point, we tend to consider this smell as applying to the "units" from which the run-time classes are specified. For example, if a small class includes a large module, the *specification* of the class is still small. Thus, the **Large Module** smell is mostly about the flexibility of the code as written.

F. The principal reason for the difference is that Java relies on static typing. In Ruby and Smalltalk, any message can be sent to any object, whereas Java attempts to prevent illegal messages at compile time. In Java, one cannot treat just any object as an array, but in Smalltalk any object can receive at:. The set of interrelated interfaces required in order for Java's Object class to support many of the methods available in Ruby or Smalltalk is hard to imagine, and may not even be achievable without the introduction of multiple inheritance.

The other main reason is that Java has language entities that are not objects, such as ints and arrays. Many functions that manipulate these entities have no obvious home, and therefore live as **Utility Function**s in various libraries. Whereas in Ruby and Smalltalk, the same concepts are implemented as proper objects, so those utility functions can be methods. Inevitably, some of them will migrate up the class hierarchy and become methods available to every object.

The other impact of having primitives such as int in a language is that the language itself must then support for loops and the like. In Ruby and Smalltalk, these procedural constructs can be replaced by methods on Fixnum, for example. Again, over time some of these methods will migrate up the class hierarchy.

Exercise 5.4: Smells and Refactorings

   A. Comments

   B. Large Module

   C. Long Method

   D. Long Parameter List

   B - Duplicate Observed Data

   B - Extract Class

   A or C - Extract Method

   B - Extract Subclass

   A - Introduce Assertion

   D - Introduce Parameter Object

   D - Preserve Whole Object

   A - Rename Method

   D - Replace Parameter with Method

Exercise 5.5: Triggers

   A. Everybody's list will be different. **Long Method** and **Comments** are the two we see most. Of those, **Long Method** is probably the one we inflict on ourselves the most.

   B. For these "measurable" smells, you can give yourself a cutoff number that tells you to review what you're doing. For example, we check twice if a method exceeds about five lines, and we question any comments in the body of a method. Define your own triggers, and consider writing automated self-checking tests that check them; the Reek tool listed in Appendix B, "Ruby Refactoring Tools," comes with a Rake task and Rspec helpers to make this easier.

Names

Exercise 6.1: Names

`add_item(item)` - Type Embedded in Name

`do_it` - Okay for a very generic operation but borders on Uncommunicative Name

`get_nodes_array` - Type Embedded in Name

`get_data` - Uncommunicative Name (perhaps)

`make_it` - Uncommunicative Name (perhaps)

`multiply_int_int(int1, int2)` - Type Embedded in Name

`process_item` - Type Embedded in Name and probably Uncommunicative Name

`sort` - Okay

`spin` - Okay (depending on the domain)

Exercise 6.2: Critique the Names

If there's an area of personal taste, it's probably in names. Your answer may well differ from this.

A. `clear` or `erase` both sound okay (depending on whatever the library or other code uses); `delete_all` seems clunky; `wash` might be okay for a pane-of-glass simulation, but seems strained for this purpose.

B. `push` is traditional; `add` is probably okay if that's what everything else in the collection library is using; `insert` is misleading, because stacks don't put items in the middle; `add_to_front` is odd as well (we think of queues having fronts but stacks having tops).

C. `cut` implies that the text is saved somewhere for pasting; `delete` is probably best; `clear` and `erase` may be okay but sound like they might apply to the whole document.

D. `compare`, `identical_to`, and `matches` are all missing a "?" at the end of their names. Although not mandatory, standards such as that help the reader navigate and understand code more quickly.

   `identical_to` is reasonable; `matches` could work, but carries a little baggage suggesting it might be a pattern match; `compare` doesn't tell us what type of result to expect, or which way the answer will come out. `eql?` opens up a whole different can of worms, implying definitions for `==`, `!=`, `hash`, and so on.

Exercise 6.3: Superclasses

Here are our suggestions; you may have found others:

A. Vehicle

B. Printer

Exercise 6.4: Method Names

A. The name `add_course` now seems inappropriate. You should rename the method to better reflect what it now does—or simplify the name to just `add`.

B. Depending on the relationship between Graph and Point, you might try any of these:

- `graph.link(p1, p2)`
- `point.link_to(other_point)`

Unnecessary Complexity

Exercise 7.2: Today versus Tomorrow

A. Forces that make it better to design for only today's requirements today:

- It's cheaper for now to do only today's design.

- We are not committed to requirements evolving in a particular direction (so we don't have to backtrack).

- We are not required to maintain tomorrow's code today.

- Code is easier to understand when it does as little as it needs to.

B. Forces that make it better to design for tomorrow's requirements today:

- It may be easier to fully flesh out the class while it's still fresh in our mind today.

- Developing for tomorrow's needs may help us understand today's needs better.

    It all comes down to a bet: On average, will it be cheaper to do only today's design and deal with tomorrow when it comes, or do the generalized designs pay for themselves by being right often enough?

    Gordon Bell, one of the great hardware designers, said, "The cheapest, fastest, and most reliable components of a computer system are those that aren't there." (Quoted in Jon Bentley's *More Programming Pearls* [7].)

Exercise 7.3: Extraction Trade-Offs

A. In general, we believe that smaller pieces are better. Indeed, the fact that our code is composed of small, loosely coupled pieces is what keeps down its long-term cost of ownership. We have responded to the needs of today's code, and one beneficial side-effect is that we have a more flexible design for the future. This is therefore not **Speculative Generality**.

B. If the reverse process of inlining the pieces would create **Long Methods** or **Large Modules** again, the current (refactored) state of the code is preferable.

C. Be sure to use names that are pertinent to the task at hand, and not too general or abstract.

Exercise 7.4: Formatting Names

A. Symptoms of **Greedy Method**:

   (a) The method's name hints that it may be *calculating* and *outputting* the person's name.

   (b) The method's parameters are completely unrelated to each other—out is related to the run-time environment, whereas person is from the application's domain.

   (c) The method is a **Utility Function**—it needs those disparate parameters to provide all of its working context.

B. Begin by untangling the two parameters. In this case, construct the full name and then write it out in one go:

```
def display_full_name(out, person)
  full_name = person.first + ' '
  if person.middle != nil
    full_name += person.middle + ' '
  end
  full_name += person.last
  out.write(full_name)
end
```

We now have a clear case of **Feature Envy**, so use *Extract Method* and *Move Method* to push the envious code onto Person:

```
def display_full_name(out, person)
  out.write(person.full_name)
end
```

Finally, we might question the need for this method at all.

Exercise 7.5: Procedural Code

A. Your solution should be similar to this:

```
class Cart
  def total_price
    @items.inject(0) { |sum, item| sum + item.price }
  end
end
```

B. The original version of cart collects the total prices of the items and adds them together to compute their total.

C. Here's our solution (yours may differ slightly). First, we gather the prices:

```ruby
class Cart
  def total_price
    prices = @items.collect { |item| item.price }
    total = 0
    prices.each { |price| total += price }
    return total
  end
end
```

Next, we borrow a neat hack from the Ruby Extensions project allowing us to convert any symbol into a `Proc`:

```ruby
class Symbol
  def to_proc
    proc { |obj, *args| obj.send(self, *args) }
  end
end
```

(`to_proc` is so generally useful that it may even be part of the standard Ruby distribution by the time you read this.) The fact that Ruby calls `to_proc` on any object passed with a `'&'` marker allows us to simplify the collection of the item prices:

```ruby
class Cart
  def total_price
    prices = @items.collect(&:price)
    total = 0
    prices.each { |price| total += price }
    return total
  end
end
```

Now we can use `Array`'s new `reduce` method (since Ruby version 1.8.7) to sum the prices:

```ruby
class Cart
  def total_price
    @items.collect(&:price).reduce(:+)
  end
end
```

D. Although this second version involved the use of a helper method, we find it easier to work with than either the original or the first refactored version—mostly because we have decoupled the collection of prices from the summing.

Duplication

Exercise 8.1: Rakefile

A. The file contains these groups of duplicated Strings:

- The names of the files to be published
- The names of the target host and source directory
- The name of the touch file

Each of these is a **Repeated Value**.

B. For the touch file we created a constant; for the host name we used *Extract Method* on the publishing step; and for the filenames we created a hash relating each file to its destination and looped over it to create a task for each:

```
require 'rake/contrib/sshpublisher'
PUBLISHED_MARKER = '.published'
PUBLICATIONS = {
  'sparky.html' => '/var/www/tools',
  'sparky.rb' => '/usr/lib/cgi-bin'
}

def publish(file, remote_dir)
  Rake::SshFilePublisher.new('www.ruby-refactoring.com',
      remote_dir, '.', file).upload
end

PUBLICATIONS.each do |src, dest|
  file PUBLISHED_MARKER => src do
    publish(src, dest)
  end
end

desc "copy all files to the live deploy locations"
task :publish => PUBLISHED_MARKER do
  touch PUBLISHED_MARKER
end
```

Exercise 8.2: Two Libraries

A. One strategy:
- Define a new logger whose interface is compatible with the Ruby 1.8 logger. It could be a simplified "layer" interface or a class with a compatible interface (that in the future would be a subclass of the Ruby 1.8 Logger), or it might be a straightforward implementation of the new class.

- Make the old loggers call the new logger.
- Modify Log and its callers to become like the new logger, so you can delete the Log class.
- Modify Logger to become like the new logger, so you can delete the Logger too.

There will be a temptation to do this relatively slowly, to use the new logger for new and changed code. Note that this adds to our conceptual burden. You might be able to use automated support to make it easier.

Exercise 8.3: Environment Variables

A. Use *Extract Method* to pull out a method that looks up the environment variable, converts it to an integer, and validates it as positive. (Do this in steps: first, second, and third copies.)

You might decide that it's okay to set `monitor_time` and `departure_offset` even if the exception will be thrown. This reduces the need for temporary variables.

You might then extract a separate method to enforce the modulo restriction.

The end result might look like this:

```
module Timer
    def integer(env, key)
      value = env[key]
      raise "#{key} missing" if value.nil?
      result = Integer(value)
      raise "#{key} should be > 0" unless result > 0
      result
    end

    def multiple(env, key, interval)
      result = integer(env, key)
      raise "#{key} should be multiple of interval" \
        unless result % interval == 0
      result
    end

    def times(env)
      check_interval = integer(env, 'interval')
      monitor_time = multiple(env, 'duration', check_interval)
      departure_offset = multiple(env, 'departure', check_interval)
      [check_interval, monitor_time, departure_offset]
    end
end
```

Micah Martin points out that this exposes two methods we'd rather were private (`integer` and `multiple`), and passes `env` and `check_interval` multiple times; he suggests extracting a class to encapsulate this.

Exercise 8.4: Template

A. Duplication:

- The whole thing is two nearly identical copies, one for `%CODE%` and one for `%ALTCODE%`. Note that one case writes to a string and the other to an output stream.

- The numeric literal 6 is a **Derived Value** based on the string literal `%CODE%`; likewise `%ALTCODE%` and 9.

- The construction of the resulting final string for each part is similar: appending a prefix, body, and suffix.

- The whole process of substituting a substring is a **Reinvented Wheel**, because the String method `sub` already does the job.

B. Remove duplication:

- Use *Extract Method* to separate the template substitutions from the printing. Self-checking tests can now be written.

- Use *Substitute Algorithm* to call String's `sub` method instead.

C. The `string.new` calls are redundant.

Your resulting code should look something like this:

```
def template(source, req_id)
  altcode = req_id[0..4] + "-" + req_id[5..7]
  return source.sub(/%CODE%/, req_id).sub(/%ALTCODE%/, altcode)
end
```

Exercise 8.5: Duplicate Observed Data

A. The duplication is often not as dramatic as it first appears. Often, the domain object has its own representation, and the widget ends up holding a string or other display representation. The advantages of this arrangement are

- The user interface is usually one of the most volatile parts of a program, whereas the domain classes tend to be modified less often (during development).

- Putting the domain information in the widget ties them together. A domain class should be able to change its value independently of whether the value is displayed on the screen. (See the Observer pattern.)

- Mixing domain and screen classes makes the domain depend on its presentation; this is backward. It's better to have them separate so the domain classes can be used with an entirely different presentation.

B. The performance can go either way. When they're in one object, the domain class updates its value using widget methods. This is typically slower as it must take into account buffering, screen updating, and so on.

On the other hand, the synchronization can become relatively costly. On some occasions, you have to find a way to make this notification cheaper. Sometimes, a domain class can avoid notifiying a widget about events that don't affect it.

Exercise 8.6: Ruby Libraries

A. Examples:

- There are dozens of graphics libraries, each offering a binding to a different underlying graphics engine.

- There are numerous ways of working with HTTP, both in the standard distribution and in the Ruby Application Archive (http://raa.ruby-lang.org/). Similarly for CGI.

- The Logger and log4r libraries.

- Many core and standard modules and classes offer aliases for certain methods— for example, Enumerable offers both `map` and `collect`—the same method with two different names.

B. Reasons for the duplication:

- The most common reason seems to be that old chestnut—historical reasons. Ruby's developers are understandably reluctant to change published interfaces that many people depend on. Instead of changing things, they add more, even if it overlaps in intent or code.

- In something as big as Ruby's libraries, there are many people working on them, and they don't always coordinate well enough to realize that they've duplicated work.

- Synonyms provide compatibility with similar functionality in other languages. It's cheap to offer a synonym for a method, so it can be tempting to help developers transition to Ruby by providing them with familiar APIs.

- The Ruby libraries are open source, and some early libraries are no longer maintained by their original creators. Later, when someone finds a defect or a shortfall in one of those libraries, it can seem easier and quicker to simply start over and create a new library.

Exercise 8.7: Points

A. Both are using points that wrap around the maxX and maxY values.

B. Use *Substitute Algorithm* to make both classes calculate wrapping the same way. Then use *Extract Class* to pull out a WrappingPoint class.

C. The search for duplication can help you identify these situations. You can create a test that reveals the defect in the bad code. While you fix it, you can drive toward similarity to the good code and then use the refactorings that address duplication to clean up the duplication.

Exercise 8.8: XML Report

A. Both methods return a string of the form `<tag>value</tag>`. In addition, we have **Inconsistent Names** for the conversion methods, and inconsistencies in the styles for string manipulation and returning a value.

B. First, harmonize the inconsistencies just noted; then extract a `value` method on each class to harmonize the middle part of each calculation. (At this point, you need to decide what to do with the `newlines`; we decided to adopt the convention that they were part of the value.) From here, you can go a few ways:

- Using *Form Template Method,* create a common ReportNode superclass and make ReportRow and ReportColumn subclasses of it. Extract `tagname` methods to return `row` and `column`, respectively. The two `to_xml` methods are now identical, so you can use *Push Up Method* to move them into ReportNode.

- Create a helper class NodeFormatter, with a method `to_xml(tagname, value)`. Update the two `to_xml` methods so that they each call this method.

- Use *Form Template Method* as above, but put the template `to_xml` method in a NodeFormatter mix-in module.

Inheritance is a more rigid relationship between classes than is delegation. The decision to use the helper class is somewhat hidden inside the clients' methods, so changing that decision will not have ripple effects onto the clients of ReportRow and ReportColumn. Creation of the superclass or the mix-in fixes the interface of both original classes and may make it harder to change them independently.

However, the helper class has no state—in fact, `to_xml` could be written as a class method. This fact would cause us to choose the superclass approach, which is more "object oriented."

Conditional Logic

Exercise 9.1: Null Object

A. An empty string may not be the right choice for a default value in every context.

B. It's possible that extracting a new class for `Bin` might give you the needed flexibility.

C. After extracting the `Bin` class, we defined a Null Object by introducing a Singleton and a "singleton method":

```
NO_BIN = Bin.new("")
def NO_BIN.report(out) end
```

Exercise 9.2: Conditional Expression

A. Your solution should look something like this:

```
if (score <= 700) &&
   ((income < 40000) || (income > 100000) ||
   !authorized || (score <= 500)) &&
   (income <= 100000)
   reject
else
   accept
end
```

B. Your solution should look something like this:

```
has_high_score = score > 700
has_low_score = score <= 500
has_high_income = income > 100000
has_mid_income = income >= 40000 && !has_high_income

if !(has_high_score ||
   (has_mid_income && authorized && !has_low_score) ||
   has_high_income)
   reject
else
   accept
end
```

C. Your solution should look something like this:

```
if score > 700
   accept
elsif (income >= 40000) && (income <= 100000) &&
   authorized && (score > 500)
   accept
elsif income > 100000
   accept
```

```
   else
      reject
   end
```

D. Your solution should look something like this:

```
def acceptable(score, income, authorized)
   return true if score > 700 || income > 100000
   return false if score <= 500 || income < 40000
   return authorized
end

if acceptable(income, score, authorized)
   accept
else
   reject
end
```

E. Possibly the most readable solution would be D-with-B, using variables or constants within `acceptable` to give names to the various ranges. Unit tests of this algorithm could also contribute to readability.

F. This table is a literal derivation from the code:

	High Income		Medium Income		Low Income	
	Auth=Y	Auth=N	Auth=Y	Auth=N	Auth=Y	Auth=N
High Score	Accept	Accept	Accept	Accept	Accept	Accept
Mid Score	Accept	Accept	Accept	Reject	Reject	Reject
Low Score	Accept	Accept	Reject	Reject	Accept	Reject

Or, alternatively:

	High Income	Medium Income	Low Income
High Score	Accept	Accept	Accept
Mid Score	Accept	Accept iff Authorized	Reject
Low Score	Accept	Reject	Reject

Exercise 9.3: Case Statement

A. If this were all there were to it, you might not bother eliminating the switch. But it would already be very natural to have `print` and `do` methods on operations, to let us eliminate the type field.

B. Here are some possibilities; you may have others:

- If a case is doing something simple, in one place, you may not feel the need to introduce separate classes.

- Case statements are especially common in places that interface with non-object-oriented parts of the system. Michael Feathers says, "I'm okay with switches if they convert data into objects." If you model your application using Alistair Cockburn's *Hexagonal Architecture* [9], you'll find this is most often true within the Adapters.

- A single `case` statement is sometimes used in a Factory or Abstract Factory. (For more information, see Gamma et al.'s *Design Patterns* [16].)

- Sometimes a `case` statement is used in several related places to control a state machine. It may make sense as is, but refactoring to the State pattern (see *Design Patterns* [16]) is often more appropriate.

Exercise 9.5: Factory Method

A. Your solution will look something like this:

```
def make_driver
  case @type
    when USE_MEMORY_DRIVER
      return MemoryDriver.new
    when USE_DEBUG_DRIVER
      return DebugDriver.new
    when USE_PRODUCTION_DRIVER
      return ProductionDriver.new
  end
end
```

B. This design contains some duplication, because the values in the enumerated list must be kept in step with the subclasses of `Driver`—in a sense the constants are **Derived Values**. If there were only two subclasses of `Driver` we'd likely say it's acceptable, but three or more and we're getting nervous.

Also, the constructor parameter `type`—and hence also the instance variable `@type`—is an example of **Control Coupling**.

C. We could use the actual subclasses of `Driver` instead of explicit constants. The code might look something like this:

```
class DriverFactory
  def initialize(klass)
    unless Class === klass && Driver > klass
      raise(ArgumentError, "must be a subclass of Driver")
    end
    @klass = klass
  end

  def make_driver
```

```
    @klass.new
  end
end
```

D. Some advantages to using the driver classes as constants:

- The code is simpler (no conditional logic, a single place where each class is instantiated).
- The code has fewer direct dependencies (doesn't name the actual driver classes).
- The delivered code can be smaller (it's no longer necessary to deliver the debugging driver class if nothing depends on it directly).
- New driver classes could be installed without having to edit the factory.

E. Some disadvantages to this new arrangement:

- The configuration is trickier; an incorrect name or a bad RUBYLIB or $: can leave the system unable to run.

Data

Exercise 10.1: Alternative Representations

Here are some implementations we came up with; you may have others:

A. Money (based on U.S. currency, where 100 cents = 1 dollar, and a cent [a penny] is the smallest coin):
- Integer count of cents.
- A Float.
- You may have to track fractions of pennies. (Some money is managed in terms of 1/10 cent.)
- String.

B. Position (in a list):
- Integer.
- If there's only one position of interest, you might manage *the* list (as seen from outside) via two lists, one containing what comes before the position and the second containing what comes after the position.
- The item at that position.

C. Range:
- First and last index.
- First index and length.

D. Social Security Number (government identification number: "123-45-6789"):

- String.

- Integer.

- Three integers.

E. Telephone number:

- String.

- Integer.

- Two numbers: area code and local number.

- Three numbers: area code, exchange, and last 4 digits.

This only considers U.S. phone numbers; it will be more complicated if you add international phone number support. You also may have to support extensions.

F. Street Address ("123 E. Main Street"):

- String.

- Multiple fields.

- Physical coordinates.

- Standardized address (standard abbreviations).

- Index in a standard list of addresses.

G. ZIP (postal) code:

- String.

- Integer.

- Two integers (U.S. post codes now use "ZIP+4" or "12345-6789").

- Index in a standard list of codes.

Exercise 10.2: Primitives and Middle Men

A. Wrapping the primitive is a two-stage process: First, create the new class and name it for the missing domain concept; and second, look for examples of **Feature Envy** and pull methods onto the new class. This second step adds behavior to the new object and thereby prevents it being a simple **Middle Man**.

Exercise 10.3: Rails Accounts

A. Almost every class, module, and view in our application knows that we are using an integer to represent money. This is an **Open Secret**, and it's beginning to get in the way.

We could fix this by introducing a Money class. For example, the to_money helper method would become to_s on Money.

Alternatively, we could use the existing Money plug-in for Rails.

Exercise 10.4: Long Parameter List

A. Many of the parameters go together in pairs to make Points. The pairs [startDegrees, endDegrees] and [arcStart, arcEnd] look like Ranges. And the first four parameters to each method define Rectangles.

B. In some ways, it's a reflection of an attempt to make a class more generic—pass in everything it could work with. Things like graphics tend to want to be "stateless," and using lots of parameters can help them do that.

It could also reflect an attempt to remain faithful to the underlying library. When users are familiar with one set of parameters, any change can present a barrier to adoption of the new library. In such cases, it seems reasonable to provide a "faithful" API, perhaps with an optional "cleaned-up" wrapper API sitting on top.

Exercise 10.5: A Counter-Argument

It depends on what's happening between the screen and the database. If it's truly a form-filling application, to get this field from the screen into that field on the database, we might not use an object-oriented approach. But as more functions are added that concern ZIP codes (validation, computing shipping distances, mapping routes, etc.), we'd expect more benefit from the object-oriented approach.

Exercise 10.6: Editor

A. "a"

B. "(". That is, we might like positions that remember where they are, even if text is inserted in front of them. For example, an editor for programmers might track the position of each method definition.

C. Instead of handing out "dead" integers, hand out Position objects, but let the editor own them. When text changes, the editor updates the Positions. The holders of the objects aren't aware of that; they just know that they can get one, or hand it back to move to a prior position.

D. Memento uses an "opaque" object: In this case, the editor may know what's inside but clients definitely don't. The client can't manipulate the Memento directly, but must hand it back to the main object to use it.

Exercise 10.7: Library Classes

abort_on_exception and priority are methods that simulate instance variables, and consequently they reveal nothing about Thread's implementation. (It is possible, though, that presenting control variables at the class interface could encourage violations of the *Law of Demeter.*)

Exercise 10.8: Hidden State

A. The objects in a Set could be held in a Hash, or directly in some form of balanced tree. The state of an immutable DateTime could be stored as a set of values (year, month, day, etc.), or as an integer count (seconds or microseconds since some event), or it could even be stored as text.

B. Because clients have no direct access to the fields, they can't change an instance behind that object's "back" (without going through its methods).

C. By completely hiding the internal organization of the object's state, we are free to experiment with data structures and algorithms until we find the best solutions for our application's needs.

Exercise 10.9: Proper Names

A. Person is a **Data Class**.

B. Client 1 produces a string in first-name-first format; clients 2, 3, and 4 produce a last-name-first string. Put methods on Person for these two variants. The attr_ accessors can then be removed to make the instance variables fully private.

```
class Person
  def initialize(last, first, middle)
    @last = last
    @first = first
    @middle = middle
  end

  def full_name
    midpart = @middle.nil? ? '' : @middle + ' '
    "#{@first} #{midpart}#{@last}"
  end

  def citation_name
    midpart = @middle.nil? ? '' : ' ' + @middle
    "#{@last}, #{@first}#{midpart}"
  end

end
```

C. It will be easier to handle these changes once the duplication is consolidated.

Exercise 10.10: Checkpoints

A. `@state` is a **Temporary Field**.

B. One approach is to create a new class `Checkpoint` to wrap the hash of values. Have `var_values` return a `Checkpoint` object, and then move the `changes` method onto that object. You may want to rename some methods too.

C. The original smell wasn't particularly bad; but the redesign does seem to be a better approach.

Inheritance

Exercise 11.1: ArrayQueue

A. This is a case of **Implementation Inheritance**. In a queue, items are added to the back and later processed by removing them from the front. But by offering the entire public interface of class `Array`, `ArrayQueue` allows its clients to insert and remove items anywhere in the list. The *class invariant* of `ArrayQueue` cannot be enforced.

Note that some clients of `ArrayQueue` may need to iterate over the queue's items— for example, to format them for display. In this case, it would appear that `ArrayQueue` needs to inherit some of the features of `Array`; but in fact these could be acquired by implementing an `each` method and then including the `Enumerable` module as a mix-in.

B. *Use Replace Inheritance with Delegation*—see Exercise 12.3 for one possible solution.

Exercise 11.2: Relationships

Our answer looks like this:

	Inheritance	Delegation	Module Inclusion
Flexibility	–	✓	✓
Communicaion	✓	–	✓
Testability	✓	–	✓

Exercise 11.3: Read-Only Documents

A. Here are some possible solutions (you may have found others):

(a) Use *Replace Inheritance with Delegation,* so that `ReadonlyDocument` becomes an Adapter for `Document`:

```ruby
class ReadonlyDocument
  extend Forwardable

  def initialize(doc); @doc = doc; end

  def_delegators :@doc, :find, :author, :numpages, :title
end
```

(b) Invert the inheritance relationship, so that only the subclass publishes the methods that can modify the object:

```ruby
class ReadonlyDocument
private
  attr_writer :title, :author
  def delete(pos, length) ...
  def insert(pos, text) ...
public
  attr_reader :numpages
  def find(regex) ...
end

class Document < ReadonlyDocument
  public :delete, :insert, :title=, :author=
end
```

(c) Use *Extract Module* to create a shared namespace for all of the paraphernalia of an editable document:

```ruby
module EditableDocument
  attr_reader :numpages
  attr_writer :title, :author
  def delete(pos, length) ...
  def insert(pos, text) ...
  def find(regex) ...
end

class ReadonlyDocument
  include EditableDocument
  private :delete, :insert, :title=, :author=
end

class Document
  include EditableDocument
end
```

B. In terms of communication, approach (c) is unnatural: An "editable document" seems to be a reasonable domain abstraction, and so is much better represented as a class rather than a module. Similarly, the inverted hierarchy of approach (b) requires some explanation—perhaps in the form of **Comments**—in order to be readily understandable.

In terms of usability, each of these designs has the same drawback: Clients of Read-onlyDocument receive an exception if they try to invoke any of the refused methods. Even if we implement those methods so that they gracefully do nothing, the LSP would still be violated (inserting text wouldn't change the document's length, for example). On balance, we have a slight preference for approach (a)—although in this case we might choose not to fix the **Refused Bequest** at all.

Finally, if the clients of these classes are close to the user interface, we do have an additional option: Instead of calling the refused methods directly, we could ask the document—whichever type it is—to post all its available Command objects on the user interface. Thus, an editable `Document` would post objects that could call `insert` and so forth, whereas a `ReadonlyDocument` would omit them. The end user could thus never invoke a code path that would call a refused method.

Responsibility

Exercise 12.1: Feature Envy

A. Give `Machine` and `Robot` their own `report` methods.

B. Now both `Machine` and `Robot` know a little bit about the format of the report; if that format ever changes we'll have a case of **Shotgun Surgery**. Another way to look at it is to say that `Machine` and `Robot` are now both somewhat **Greedy Module**s.

C. We can't think of a good way to remove all the smells here. On balance, we would leave the **Feature Envy** in place:

- We think of the `Report` as a *View* of the domain objects: One way or another it needs to know about their relationships and their state, because that's its job.

- The details of the `Report` are likely to change more frequently than those of `Machine` and `Robot`, which represent objects in the application's real world. We prefer to keep different rates of change—and different reasons for change—separate.

Exercise 12.2: Walking a List

A. `Agency` knows that `Theater` has split the occupancy string into an array of markers, and it also knows the values of those markers. Knowledge of these implementation decisions has been duplicated, creating unnecessary coupling in the design.

B. Use *Extract Method* to isolate the calculation of `free_seats`, then use *Move Method* to push that code into `Theater`.

Exercise 12.3: Middle Man

A. Removing the **Middle Man** is probably not an improvement. The SimpleQueue class provided two benefits: First, the class name and the method names communicate intent, and thereby help to document any application using them. And second, a SimpleQueue cannot be confused with an Array, because it doesn't support the same methods. SimpleQueue is thus an Adapter (see Gamma's *Design Patterns* [16]) that serves to decouple parts of the design from each other, which in turn helps to limit the effects of change.

Exercise 12.4: Cart

B. Add `cost` and `days` methods to Purchase.

C. Cart no longer needs access to `item` and `shipping` on `Purchase`. So hiding the delegate widens the interface as we create methods for related objects, but it may let us narrow the interface as the client doesn't need to navigate any more.

D. Remove the `attr_reader` declarations for `item` and `shipping`.

E. In this case, the order we change these probably doesn't make a whole lot of difference.

Exercise 12.5: Utility Functions

A. For Exercise 5.1, we would probably extend Array with `clip` and `delta?` methods:

```
class Array
  def clip(limit)
    map { |val| [val, limit].min }
  end

  def delta?(expected, delta)
    !self.zip(expected).detect { |m|
    (m[0] - m[1]).abs > delta
    }
  end
end
```

Then we can move some of the code out of `Matcher`, thus:

```
class Matcher
  def self.match(expected, actual, clip_limit, delta)
    actual.length == expected.length and
    actual.clip(clip_limit).delta?(expected, delta)
  end
end
```

To complete the fix, we might consider moving the match method onto Array too, although it doesn't sit well as a function of general arrays. So, depending on other factors in this part of the application, we might be tempted to introduce a new class for actual.

B. In a larger application, we might decide that there's a missing Warehouse class to hold the line and the Robot; it would then be sensible for report to be an instance method on the Warehouse.

Exercise 12.6: Attributes

A. Here are some counterexamples we found; you may have others:

- Some mechanisms—ActiveRecord, for example—use reflection to enable them to manipulate objects irrespective of their class.

- When you're trying to get a hairy piece of legacy code under test, often a good starting point is to expose an instance variable to act as a "probe" point (Michael Feathers, *Working Effectively with Legacy Code* [10]).

B. Structs are a nice convenience when you need to create a class in a hurry, and they clearly document the fact that you decided not to give the class any behavior at this time. But unless the conditions above apply, we soon look for ways to replace the Struct by a Class and add methods to it.

Exercise 12.7: Message Chains

A. Each of these code fragments violates the Law of Demeter, because they each call a method on an object that was returned from another call.

B. Only the second fragment is a **Message Chain**. In the first, a new array is created by each method, so there is no sense of navigating from object to object. In the third example, we have a Cascade or DSL, and most of the messages return self.

Accommodating Change

Exercise 13.1: CSV Writer

A. One decision is *where* to write; the other decision is *how* to write.

B. Simply adding an io argument to every method in CsvWriter creates a lot of duplicated parameter lists. This could be relieved by passing the IO object to CsvWriter's constructor.

C. Here's our solution:

```ruby
class CsvFormatter

  def format(lines)
    lines.collect { |line| write_line(line) }.join("\n")
  end

private

def write_line(fields)
    fields.collect { |field| write_field(field) }.join(",")
  end

  def write_field(field)
    case field
      when /,/ then quote_and_escape(field)
      when /"/ then quote_and_escape(field)
    else field
    end
end

  def quote_and_escape(field)
    "\"#{field.gsub(/\"/, "\"\"")}\""
  end
end

require 'csv_formatter'
require 'test/unit'

class CsvFormatterTest < Test::Unit::TestCase

  def setup
    @csv = CsvFormatter.new
  end

  def test_no_lines
    assert_equal("", @csv.format([]))
  end

  def test_no_quotes_or_commas
    assert_equal("", @csv.format([[]]))
    assert_equal("only one field",
      @csv.format([["only one field"]]))
    assert_equal("two,fields",
      @csv.format([["two", "fields"]]))
    assert_equal(",contents,several words included",
      @csv.format([["", "contents", "several words included"]]))
```

```
      assert_equal("two\nlines",
        @csv.format([["two"], ["lines"]]))
  end

  def test_commas_and_quotes
    assert_equal('","","embedded , commas","trailing,"',
      @csv.format([[',', 'embedded , commas', 'trailing,']]))
    assert_equal('""""","multiple """"" quotes"""""',
      @csv.format([['"', 'multiple """ quotes""']]))
    assert_equal('"commas, and ""quotes""",simple',
      @csv.format([['commas, and "quotes"', 'simple']]))
  end
end
```

D. Call the original "Version A," the `IO` one "Version B," and the string one "Version C." Version B can be tested by passing in a `StringIO` object (see Ruby's standard library). Version C offers more flexibility because of the central role played by Strings throughout Ruby's design. Version C can simulate Version B through simple idioms such as:

```
$stdout << CsvFormatter.new.write(lines)
```

Conversely, Version B can simulate Version C:

```
strio = StringIO.new
CsvWriter.new.write(lines, strio)
s = strio.string
```

Thus, Version B is more cumbersome in all but a very few applications.

Exercise 13.3: Hierarchies in Rails

We don't see a smell here: Models and views/controllers will experience different pressures for change during the application's development. The one-to-one correspondence between controllers and models is a convention established by the generators to help you get a Rails application up and running quickly. Later, as the views evolve, it is likely that the controllers and models will drift apart.

Exercise 13.4: Documents

A. It affects places all over the class hierarchy.

B. Whether it is an improvement depends on how it will be used. We don't have enough information to judge at this stage.

C. The brief/full and compression/none distinctions will become the *wrapping* types.

Libraries

Exercise 14.1: Layers

A. UML package diagram:

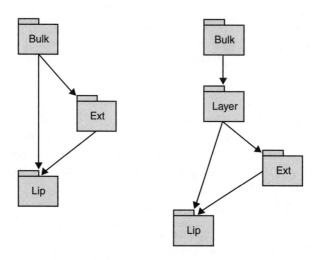

B. In the first case, the bulk of your code depends directly on the library.

In the second case, it depends directly on the layer, and only indirectly on the library. However, design choices in the layer may still mean that your code depends subtly on the library—in terms of the use of primitive types, for example. Look out for examples of **Open Secrets** among the various modules involved.

C. *Conceptual integrity.* It depends. A good layer interface can improve the way we think about things.

   Portability. Better; changes may be concentrated in the layer.

   Performance. It can go either way. There's a small cost to going through the layer, but the layer may be able to cache data or otherwise speed up performance.

   Testing. It may be easier to test in the layer, especially if the layer's interface is narrower. It may make it easier to swap in a test implementation as well.

D. Ruby doesn't have language mechanisms to enforce it. You might have external mechanisms (e.g., a tool that checks references to the layered packages.)

Exercise 14.2: Closed Classes

A. The ability to redefine the methods of any class means that developers could alter their standard meanings. Worse, existing tested production code could be subverted by a few careless keystrokes.

Agile development approaches rely on the premise that many aspects of an application will quickly stabilize, even when the requirements themselves are fluid. Part of the speed of these approaches comes from being able to rely on the correctness of increasingly large core parts of the application. But if just one developer on the team has the habit of customizing core classes to enforce local convention or personal whim, the cost-of-change curve will shoot back up and the productivity gains will be lost.

(We have seen this effect firsthand in C++ code, where an overloaded + operator did something very unexpected when applied to a Matrix; the resulting code looked straightforward, but wasted huge amounts of time until the "surprise" was uncovered.)

B. One approach is local coding standards and conventions, such as *Don't redefine methods of core classes.*

C. Calling `freeze` on any object prevents its instance variables from being changed; and applying it to a `Class` thus prevents changes to its methods:

```
class Foo
  # method definitions etc...
  freeze
end
```

However, a frozen class can still be subclassed, and the subclass is not frozen. The Ruby community is enjoying the challenge of searching for a bulletproof solution to this problem, thus far without success. It is likely that convention, coupled with trust and common sense, is the only practical way to deal with Ruby's largesse.

Exercise 14.3: Missing Function

A. In Ruby, you can simply extend the Math module with the missing method:

```
module Math
  def Math.zum(x)
    (Math.cos(x) + Math.sin(x) - Math.exp(x)).abs
  end
end
```

A Simple Game

Exercise 15.1: Smells

- **Open Secret**: The Board is represented as a String; it could be a new class.
- **Open Secret**: It might make sense to have a Player class.
- **Open Secret**: There are lots of magic numbers.
- **Complicated Boolean Expression**: There are several complicated "if" statements.
- **Duplicated Code**: There's a lot of duplication—note the winner calculation in particular.

Exercise 15.3: Fuse Loops

D. These considerations apply when merging loops:

- It's easiest if both loops have the same range.
- It's important that the ith entry of the second loop not depend on anything past the ith entry in the first loop.

Exercise 15.4: Result

The second conditional is redundant, because we return NO_MOVE even when default_move has that value. We can simplify to

```
return winning_move if winning_move != NO_MOVE
return default_move
```

Exercise 15.6: Constants

We chose

```
ROWS = 3
COLUMNS = 3
```

Exercise 15.8: Representations

A. We found at least these dependencies on the String representation:

- Everywhere in Game, references to cells on the board use the [] operator to extract a one-character substring.
- Every (original) method in both Game and the tests knows that a single integer can be used to index the cells of the board.
- The loop in best_move_for assumes that the cells can be accessed in sequence.

B. These are some possibilities (you may have found others):

- A simple Array of one-character Strings

- An Array of rows, each of which is an Array of one-character Strings

- A simple Array of Cells

- A nine-digit number (base 3 or base 10)

In code this small, the key feature is not the representation, but rather the methods that encapsulate it.

Time Recording

Exercise 16.1: Rewrite or Refactor?

A. Every situation is different. Here are some of the arguments in favor of refactoring:

- It may be necessary to offer users a gradual transition during development.

- It may be possible to retain the investment in difficult algorithms.

- Some aspects of the user interface design may have been dictated by the tools used, and may be difficult to replicate using other libraries.

And here are some arguments in favor of a rewrite from scratch:

- The existing code may be too hard to work with.

- A fresh start may lead to a simpler solution.

- A fresh start means that everyone's issues can be addressed at one go.

You may have discovered others.

B. Reek (version 1.0.0) reports the following:

```
"timelog.rb" -- 17 warnings:
[Duplication] parse_options calls argv.length multiple times
[Duplication] parse_options calls options.hours multiple times
[Duplication] report calls hours.to_f multiple times
[Duplication] report calls options.user multiple times
[Feature Envy] log refers to options more than self
[Feature Envy] report refers to options more than self
[Feature Envy] report refers to records more than self
[Long Method] parse_options has approx 18 statements
[Long Method] report has approx 13 statements
[Nested Iterators] parse_options/block/block is nested
[Uncommunicative Name] log/block has the variable name 'f'
[Uncommunicative Name] parse_options/block/block has the variable name 'd
[Uncommunicative Name] report/block has the variable name 'd'
[Uncommunicative Name] report/block has the variable name 'm'
```

```
[Uncommunicative Name] report/block has the variable name 'y'
[Utility Function] log doesn't depend on instance state
[Utility Function] report doesn't depend on instance state
```

Clearly, `report` is also a **Greedy method**.

Exercise 16.3: Test Coverage

There is no coverage of the full content of a report, and there are no explicit tests to check what happens when time is recorded. Tests for error conditions—a malformed date, for example—are also missing.

Exercise 16.6: Rates of Change

After this refactoring, we have a new class with the following signature:

```
class Logfile
  all_project_records(projectname)       # -> Array of CSV strings
  all_user_records(projectname, username) # -> Array of CSV strings
  save(csv_string)
end
```

The string representing the path to the file is a primitive, whereas the `TimelogFile` instance provides a layer of abstraction. In a sense, there is now *less* duplication, due to that weakened coupling between the application, the script, and the tests.

Exercise 16.8: Hexagonal Architecture

Figure A.1 shows one possible model. Note that the exact details are much less important than conveying the overall structure in the most minimal terms.

Exercise 16.9: Data Smells

A. The main potential problem is that there's no indication of what the keys are in each table. A good rule in table design is: Each row depends on the key, the whole key, and nothing but the key.

B. We might specify keys as follows:

- For StaffMembers: Use the `username` or add a separate ID.
- For Projects: Use the `codename` or add a separate ID.
- For Assignments: Add an ID column.

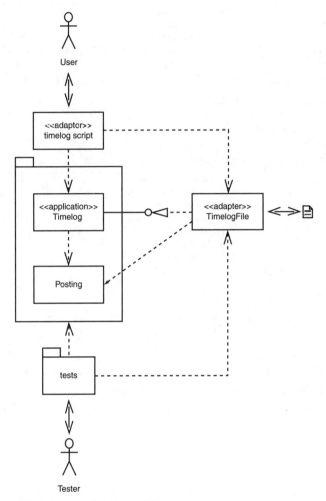

Figure A.1 The Logfile Adapter and Variation Point

Exercise 16.10: Extending the Database

Figure A.2 shows one simple extension to the database.

Exercise 16.12: Database Technology

There is a good in-depth discussion of the leading candidates in Hal Fulton's *The Ruby Way* [15]: SQLite, MySQL, PostgreSQL, Oracle, ActiveRecord.

As is often the case with technology choices, ours was made purely on the basis of what we were actively using on other projects at the time. Any other choice would

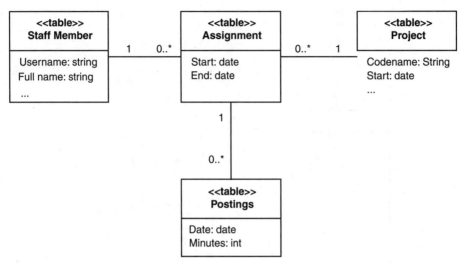

Figure A.2 Extending the Corporate Projects Database

be just as valid. And although many readers will be familiar with Rails, we did decide against using the Rails `ActiveRecord` gem, simply because this book is intended to cover Ruby in general.

So we picked MySQL. For our development environment (Ubuntu), we needed to install MySQL, followed by the `libmysql-ruby` package, and then run some tests. You may need to carry out different steps in your environment, and there's plenty of help on the Web if you need it.

Ruby Refactoring Tools

A number of refactoring tools for Ruby are now available, many in the alpha or beta stages of development. This appendix lists those we know about at the time of going to press.

Code Smell Detectors

flay   Finds code fragments with identical or similar structure:
http://ruby.sadi.st/Flay.html

flog   Computes ABC code complexity metrics for Ruby code:
http://ruby.sadi.st/Flog.html

heckle   A mutation tester; changes your code and re-runs your tests to check for coverage: http://rubyforge.org/projects/seattlerb/

Reek   Our very own open source tool identifies smells in your Ruby code:
http://wiki.github.com/kevinrutherford/reek

Roodi   Checks Ruby code against style guidelines:
http://rubyforge.org/projects/roodi

Simian   Simon Harris of RedHill has created a Rails plug-in that allows you to run Simian—the code duplication finder—from the rakefile:
http://www.redhillonrails.org/simian.html

Environments with Refactoring Support

Aptana   A complete IDE, built from Eclipse with the RADRails plug-in; offers excellent refactoring support: `http://aptana.com/`

NetBeans   Sun's rival to Eclipse; the Ruby module provides first-class refactoring tools: `http://www.netbeans.org/features/ruby/index.html`

RubyMine   JetBrains's Ruby and Rails IDE is built on the IntelliJ platform and includes refactoring support: `http://www.jetbrains.com/ruby/index.html`

Bibliography

[1] Dave Astels. *Test-Driven Development: A Practical Guide*. Prentice Hall, 2003.

[2] Kent Beck. *Smalltalk Best Practice Patterns*. Prentice Hall, 1996.

[3] Kent Beck. *Test-Driven Development: By Example*. Addison-Wesley, 2003.

[4] Kent Beck. *Extreme Programming Explained: Embrace Change, Second Edition*. Addison-Wesley, 2004.

[5] Kent Beck and Ward Cunningham. "A Laboratory for Teaching Object-Oriented Thinking." In *OOPSLA '89 Conference Proceedings*, New Orleans, Louisiana, 1989.

[6] Jon Bentley. *Programming Pearls*. Addison-Wesley, 1986.

[7] Jon Bentley. *More Programming Pearls*. Addison-Wesley, 1988.

[8] David Chelimsky, Dave Astels, Zach Dennis, Aslak Hellesoy, Bryan Helmkamp, and Dan North. *The RSpec Book: Behaviour Driven Development with RSpec, Cucumber, and Friends*. The Pragmatic Bookshelf, 2009.

[9] Mlistair Cockburn. Hexagonal architecture. `http://c2.com/cgi/wiki?Hexagonal Architecture`, 2004.

[10] Michael Feathers. *Working Effectively with Legacy Code*. Prentice Hall, 2004.

[11] Jay Fields, Shane Harvie, and Martin Fowler. *Refactoring, Ruby Edition*. Addison-Wesley, 2009.

[12] Martin Fowler. *Patterns of Enterprise Application Architecture*. Addison-Wesley, 2002.

[13] Martin Fowler. Fluent interface. `http://www.martinfowler.com/bliki/Fluent Interface.html`, 2005.

[14] Martin Fowler, Kent Beck, John Brant, William Opdyke, and Don Roberts. *Refactoring: Improving the Design of Existing Code*. Addison-Wesley, 2000.

[15] Hal Fulton. *The Ruby Way, Second Edition.* Addison-Wesley, 2006.

[16] Erich Gamma, Richard Helm, Ralph Johnson, and John Vlissides. *Design Patterns.* Addison-Wesley, 1995.

[17] Andrew Hunt and David Thomas. *The Pragmatic Programmer.* Addison-Wesley, 2000.

[18] Brian W. Kernighan and P. J. Plauger. *The Elements of Programming Style.* Computing McGraw-Hill, 1988.

[19] Leonard Koren. *Wabi-Sabi: For Artists, Designers, Poets and Philosophers.* Stone Bridge Press, 2003.

[20] Brian Marick. *Everyday Scripting with Ruby: For Teams, Testers, and You.* Pragmatic Bookshelf, 2007.

[21] Robert C. Martin. *Agile Software Development: Principles, Patterns, and Practices.* Prentice Hall, 2002.

[22] Gerard Meszaros. *xUnit Test Patterns: Refactoring Test Code.* Addison-Wesley, 2007.

[23] Bertrand Meyer. *Object-Oriented Software Construction.* Prentice Hall, 1988.

[24] Russ Olsen. *Design Patterns in Ruby.* Addison-Wesley, 2007.

[25] David Parnas. "On the Criteria to Be Used in Decomposing Systems into Modules." *Communications of the ACM,* 15(2), 1972.

[26] William C. Wake. *Refactoring Workbook.* Addison-Wesley, 2003.

Index

Footnote references are indicated with "n," followed by the footnote number.

!, 54, 219, 221
&, 224
*(), 198, 200, 209
===, 101
?, 221
[] operator, 4, 54, 246
@ symbol, 59
%ALTCODE%, 89, 227
%CODE%, 88, 227
@delegate.f, 145
@state, 122, 237

A

accept(), 103
Accessor, 29
ActionController::Base, 162
ActiveRecord, 194, 249–250
ActiveRecord::Base, 116–117, 162, 194
ActiveRecord::Migration, 115
Adapter, 164–165, 190, 192–194, 232, 237, 240, 249
Add Parameter, 85, 140
Adjectives, 57
Agile Software Development (Martin), 70, 146
Aliases, 54, 218, 228
Alpha-beta pruning, 182
Alternative Modules with Different Interfaces, 85
Alternative Representations, 115, 233–234

and, 98
And, in method names, 70
Aptana, 252
Array, 72, 108
ArrayQueue, 133, 237
Assertions, 30, 42, 55, 220
Astels, Dave, 23
at:, 219
attr, 151
attr_accessor, 110, 151, 236
Attributes, 151, 241
attr_reader, 14, 151, 240
attr_writer, 151
autotest, 26

B

BDD (behavior-driven development), 22–23
Beck, Kent, 21, 23, 26, 142, 189
Behavior-preserving transformations, 27
Bell, Gordon, 222
Bentley, Jon, 93, 222
best_move_for, 175–177, 179
binary_op, 203, 210
button_frame, 207–209, 211

C

cab(), 204, 209–210
Caching, 181

Calculator program
  `button_frame`, 207–209, 211
  `cab()`, 204, 209–210
  `Calc_Controller` class, 204
  `extend()`, 201, 204, 209, 211
  refactoring, 209–210
  source code, 197 *n*1
  stack, 197, 201–203, 209, 221
  units, 198, 200–201
  user interface, 205–206
Cart, 150–151, 240
Cascade, 143, 241
Case Statement, 104, 106, 231–232
`case` statement, 101, 232
Change-related code smells
  Combinatorial Explosion, 159
  Divergent Change, 5, 154–155, 161, 189
  Parallel Inheritance Hierarchies, 158
  Shotgun Surgery, 156–157, 162
Check (refactoring micro-process step), 30
Checkpoints, 122–123, 237
Chelimsky, David, 23
Class invariant, 237
`class_eval`, 74–75
Closed Classes, 168–169, 245
Cockburn, Alistair, 190, 232
Code coverage tool, 76
Code downloads, 18
Code reuse, 18, 133–134, 167
Code review checklist, 23
Code rewriting, 19
Code smells
  change-related, 153–162
  complexity, 65–78
  conditional logic, 93–106
  data, 107–123
  duplication, 79–92
  inheritance, 125–134
  libraries, 163–169
  measurable, 41–55
  name-related, 57–63
  as problem indicators, 20

responsibility, 135–152
  software, 23, 251–252
Code test suite, 25
Coin-toss code, 4–7
Collapse hierachy, 33, 216
`collect`, 72
Combinatorial Explosion, 159
Comma-separated value (CSV). *See* CSV
        Writer
Comments, 5, 10–11, 42–43, 49–50, 55, 217
Comparable module, 218
Compile step (of other languages), 25, 28
Complexity code smells
  Dead Code, 5–6, 66–67, 76, 209
  Dynamic Code Creation, 74–75
  Greedy Method, 5, 7–9, 70–72, 78, 189, 223
  Procedural Code, 72–73, 78, 223–224
  Speculative Generality, 68–69, 76–77, 222
Complicated Boolean Expression, 98–99, 246
Compound words, 59
Conditional Expression, 103–104, 230
Conditional logic code smells
  Complicated Boolean Expression, 98–99, 246
  Control Coupling, 100, 105, 232
  Nil Check, 94–95
  Simulated Polymorphism, 101–102, 209
  Special Case, 96–97
Configuration management, 26
Consistency, 6–7
Consolidate Conditional Expression, 103
Constants, 11, 32, 81, 177, 232–233, 246
Control Coupling, 100, 105, 232
Controller, 204–205, 210–211
Copying code, 31
Counter-Argument, 118, 235
CRC (class, responsibilities, collaborators)
        cards, 26, 135
CSV strings, 190
CSV Writer, 160–161, 241–243
`CSV::Writer`, 161
Cunningham, Ward, 26, 57
Currency, 115, 151, 233–235

Cutoff values, 182
Cycle of refactoring, 19–23

D

Data Class, 110–111, 234, 236
Data Clump, 5, 10, 112–113
Data code smells
    Data Class, 110–111, 234, 236
    Data Clump, 5, 10, 112–113
    Open Secret, 108–109, 115, 176, 190,
        233–235
    Temporary Field, 114, 146, 237
Data smells, 191, 248
Database, 186–187, 192–194, 249–250
Dead Code, 5–6, 66–67, 76, 209
Dead integers, 119, 235
Decorator design pattern, 159, 162
Defactoring practice exercise, 36–37
Default value, 81, 94, 209–210, 230
Defensive guard clause, 96, 104
Delegates and delegation
    Hide Delegate, 26–29, 33, 143–144,
        150–151, 216
    Middle Man, 115, 145, 149–151, 209, 234,
        240
    Remove Middle Man, 145, 150, 216
    Replace Delegation with Inheritance, 145,
        237
    Replace Inheritance with Delegation,
        126–127
Delete (refactoring micro-process step), 32
DeMorgan's law, 98, 103
Dependency Inversion, 167
Deprecating code, 32
Depth parameter, 181
Derived Value, 5, 15–16, 80, 227
Design patterns, 135, 145, 159, 162
Design Patterns (Gamma et al.), 232, 240
Design perfection, 17, 22
Design rules, 21–22
Design simplicity, 21, 23, 215
Development and refactoring, 22–23

Dictionaries, 57
Dimension class, 198, 209–211
Divergent Change, 5, 154–155, 161, 189
Document compression, 162
Documents, 162, 243
Domain class, 46, 89, 140, 227–228
Double Dispatch, 142
`DriverFactory`, 105–106, 232
DRY (Don't Repeat Yourself) principle, 22,
    117
DSL (domain-specific languages), 143, 241
Duplicate Observed Data, 46, 55, 89,
    227–228
Duplicated Code, 5, 83–84, 91, 209–210,
    215
Duplication and code smells, 22, 37
Dynamic Code Creation, 74–75

E

`each`, 72
`each_move` method, 179–180
Editor, 118–119, 235
Eiffel language, 61
Elements of Programming Style, The (Kernighan
    and Plauger), 93
`else`, 103
Emergent design, 20
Encapsulate Collection, 110
Enumerable, 72, 181, 218, 228, 237
Environment variables, 87–88, 226–227
`eval`, 74–75
Explicit methods, 102, 216
Explicit refusal, 128–129
`extend()`, 201, 204, 209, 211
Extract Class, 46, 55, 188, 189, 216, 220, 229
Extract Method, 31, 33, 38, 49, 55, 216, 220
Extract Module, 46, 238
Extract Subclass, 46, 55, 216, 220
Extract Superclass, 85, 154
Extraction, 77, 222
*Extreme Programming Explained, Second
    Edition* (Beck), 21

F

Factory Method, 105–106, 232–233
Feathers, Michael, 26, 232, 241
Feature Envy, 12–14, 136–137, 148, 209, 239
Fields, Jay, 33, 35, 38, 158
Flag value, 176
flay (refactoring tool), 251
FlexMock, 152
flog (refactoring tool), 251
Fluent Interface, 143
Flyweight, 109
For each (refactoring micro-process step), 31
for loops, 219
Form Template Method, 84
Formatting names, 77–78, 223
Formatting text, 218
Fowler, Martin, 19, 25, 108, 143, 194
freeze, 245
Fulton, Hal, 249
Fuse Loops, 176–177, 246

G

<g>, 16–17
Game program
code, 173–175
development episodes, 180–182
refactoring, 175–180, 246–247
source code, 173 *n*1
Gamma, Erich, 232, 240
Gems, 26, 76, 163, 167, 192
Generic refactoring micro-process, 30–32
Global Variable, 5–6, 140
Google group mailing list, 38
Gorts, Sven, 19
Greedy Method, 5, 7–9, 70–72, 78, 189, 223
Greedy Module, 5, 7, 9–10, 146–147, 209
Green bar, 22–23
Guard Clauses, 96, 104–105

H

Harmonizing practice exercise, 37
Hash, 72, 108–109, 225, 236–237

heckle (refactoring tool), 76, 251
Helper class, 44, 229
Helper methods, 117, 178, 224, 235
Hexagonal architecture, 190, 232, 248
Hidden State, 119–120, 236
Hide Delegate, 26–29, 33, 143–144, 150–151, 216
Hierarchies in Rails, 162, 243
Hooks, 66, 68, 131
HTTP wrapper, 7–8
Hungarian notation, 59
Hunt, Andrew, 143, 152

I

if, 103, 174–175, 246
if xxx == nil, 94
if xxx.nil?, 94
Implementation Inheritance, 126–127, 134, 237
Implicit refusal, 128–129
Inappropriate Intimacy (General Form), 141–142, 151, 209
Inappropriate Intimacy (Subclass Form), 130
Incomplete Library Module, 164–165
Inconsistent Names, 61, 229
Information hiding, 79
Inhale/exhale practice exercise, 36
Inheritance, 134, 229
Inheritance code smells
Implementation Inheritance, 126–127, 134, 237
Inappropriate Intimacy (Subclass Form), 130
Lazy Class, 131–132
Refused Bequest, 128–129, 134, 237–239
Inheritance Survey, 134
Inject method, 78, 223
Inline Class, 69
Inline refactoring, 69
Inline Temp, 33, 216
Instance method, 138
Instance variables, 46, 114, 119–120, 141, 152

`instance_of?`, 101
`instance_variables`, 141
`instance_variables_get`, 141
`int`, 219
Integrated Development Environment (IDE),
26, 252
Integration tests, 194
Internationalization library, 18, 61, 76, 81
Introduce (refactoring micro-process step), 31
Introduce Assertion, 42, 55, 220
Introduce Explaining Variable, 98, 103, 216
Introduce Local Extension, 164, 169
Introduce Null Object, 94, 103
Introduce Parameter Object, 49, 55, 220
Inverse refactorings, 33, 216
IO, 161, 241
`is_a?`, 101
`is_calculated`, 201–205, 210
Iterate, 31
Iterations, 72, 78
Iterator, 179–180
Iterator index, 5

J
Jar file, 164
Java, 28, 54, 219
JetBrains, 252

K
Kata refactoring practice exercise, 37
Kernighan, Brian, 93
`kind_of?`, 101
Koren, Leonard, 17

L
Large Class, 46, 51–54, 218
Large Module, 46–47, 55, 77, 220
Law of Demeter, 143, 152, 236, 241
Layers, 168, 244
Lazy Class, 131–132
Legacy code, 26, 241
Libraries, 6, 76, 81, 86–87, 90, 225–226, 228

Library Classes, 119, 236
Library code smells
Incomplete Library Module, 164–165
Reinvented Wheel, 6, 166
Runaway Dependencies, 167
`line`, 9
Liskov Substitution Principle (LSP), 128–129,
239
Local extension, 164, 169
Logfile Adapter and Variation Point, 249
`LogFile.log`, 86–87
Logger, 225–226
Long Method, 44–45, 50–51, 55, 77,
217–218, 222
Long Parameter List, 5, 10–11, 48–49, 55,
118, 220, 235
Loops, 72–73, 176–177, 246

M
Magic numbers, 81, 175, 177, 246
Mailing list for this book, 38
`make_digit()`, 207–208, 210
`make_driver`, 105–106
`make_unit()`, 207–208, 210
Malfactoring practice exercise, 36–37
Martin, Micah, 227
Martin, Robert, 70, 146
`match()`, 49, 240
Matcher, 49, 151, 217, 240
Math module, 169, 245
`maxX`, 229
`maxY`, 229
Measurable code smells
Comments, 42–43, 49–50, 55, 217
Large Module, 46–47, 55, 77
Long Method, 44–45, 50–51, 55, 77,
217–218, 222
Long Parameter List, 5, 10–11, 48–49, 55,
118, 220, 235
Member variable, 59
Memento, 110, 119, 235
Message Chain, 143–144, 152, 241

Method aliases, 54, 218, 228
Method length, 44–45, 50–51, 55, 77,
    217–218, 222
Method names, 59, 63, 221–222
Method object, 44
method_missing, 74, 94, 147
Meyer, Bertrand, 154
Middle Man, 115, 145, 149–151, 209, 216,
    234, 240
Migrate (refactoring micro-process step),
    31–32
Min-max algorithm, 182
Missing Function, 169, 245
Module inclusion, 134
Module size, 46–47, 77, 220
module_eval, 74–75
Money, 115, 151, 233–235
More Programming Pearls (Bentley), 93, 222
move, 175
Move Method, 85
MySQL, 187, 193, 249–250

N

Name formatting, 77–78, 223
Name-related code smells
    Inconsistent Names, 61, 229
    Type Embedded in Name, 59, 62,
        220–221
    Uncommunicative Name, 5, 14–15, 60, 62,
        175–176, 209, 220–221
Naming conventions and standards, 57–61
Nested iterators, 247
NetBeans, 252
new, 167
Newlines, 229
nil, 94, 103
Nil Check, 94–95, 103
NodeFormatter, 229
not, 98
Nouns, 57
Null Object, 94–95, 103, 230
Numbered variables, 60

O

OAOO (once and only once), 22
Object-Oriented Software Construction (Meyer),
    154
Open classes, 85, 168–169
Open Secret, 108–109, 115, 176, 190,
    233–235
Open source practice projects, 37–38
or, 98, 100
Oracle, 249

P

Parallel Inheritance Hierarchies, 158
Parameter lists, 11, 48–49. *See also* Long
    Parameter List
Parameter object, 49, 55, 220
Parameterize Method, 33, 85, 167, 216
Parnas, David, 79
Pattern matching, 218
Patterns of Enterprise Application Architecture
    (Fowler), 194
Perfection, 17, 22, 32
Persistence mechanisms, 110, 189, 194
Plauger, P. J., 93
play method, 178
Points, 90–91, 229
points, 12
polyline, 9–10, 12–13
Polymorphism, 96, 101–102, 209
Position objects, 119
PostgreSQL, 249
Practice skills, 35–38
Pragmatic Programmer, The (Hunt and
    Thomas), 143, 152
Preserve Whole Object, 11–12, 49, 55, 220
Primitive objects, 115, 219, 234
Primitive Obsession, 108
Probe points, 68, 241
Proc:, 224
Procedural Code, 72–73, 78, 223–224
Programming Pearls (Bentley), 93
Proper Names, 120–122, 236

Pull Up Method, 84
Push Down Method, 129
Push Up Method, 229
puts, 13

R

Rails accounts, 115–118, 234–235
Rails hierarchies, 162, 243
Rails money plug-in, 235
Rake, 220
Rakefile, 86, 225, 251
Rates of change, 189, 248
Rcov (code coverage tool), 76
rdoc API documentation, 42, 217
Re-refactoring practice exercise, 36
Read-Only Documents, 134, 237–239
rect, 8, 27
Red bar, 22–23
reduce method, 224
Reek software, 23, 247, 251
Refactoring, Ruby Edition, (Fields et al.), 33, 35, 38, 159
Refactoring (Fowler et al.), 19
Reflection transform, 15–16
Refused Bequest, 128–129, 134, 237–239
Regression suite, 23
Reinvented Wheel, 6, 166
reject, 72
Relationships, 133–134, 237–239
Remove Middle Man, 145, 150, 216
Remove Parameter, 69
Remove Setting Methods, 69
Rename Method, 33, 55, 59–60, 85, 216, 220
Repeated Value, 81–82, 225
Replace Array with Object, 109
Replace Delegation with Inheritance, 145
Replace Hash with Object, 109
Replace Inheritance with Delegation, 126–127, 129, 159, 237
Replace Loop with Collection Closure Method, 72–73

Replace Magic Number with Symbolic Constant, 81
Replace Method with Method Object, 44
Replace Parameter with Explicit Methods, 102, 216
Replace Parameter with Method, 48, 55, 220
Replace Temp with Chain, 73
Replace Value with Expression, 80
ReportColumn, 91, 229
ReportNode, 229
Report.report, 51, 148, 151, 218
ReportRow, 91, 229
require statements, 167
Responsibility code smells
    Feature Envy, 12–14
    Global Variable, 5–6, 140
    Greedy Module, 5, 7, 9–10, 146–147, 209
    Inappropriate Intimacy (General Form), 141–142, 151, 209
    Message Chain, 143–144, 152, 241
    Middle Man, 115, 145, 149–150, 209, 234, 240
    Utility Function, 5, 138–139, 151, 240–241
return statements, 176
reversed_copy, 219
ri18n internationalization library, 81
Roodi, 251
row, 178
rspec, 23, 26
RSpec Book (Chelimsky et al.) 23
Rspec examples, 51, 220
Ruby Application Archive, 228
Ruby Extensions, 224
Ruby Way, The (Fulton), 249
RubyForge, 76, 163, 251
RubyMine, 252
Run-time checks, 28
Runaway Dependencies, 167

S

Safe points, 28–29
Scavenger hunt practice exercise, 36

Secret. *See* Open Secret

`select`, 72

`self`, 136, 152

`self.class`, 136

Short names, 60

Shotgun Surgery, 156–157, 162

Simian, 251

Simplicity in design, 21, 23, 215

Simulated Polymorphism, 101–102, 209

Single Responsibility Principle (SRP), 70, 146, 176

Small steps, 33, 36, 216

Smalltalk, 54, 143, 189, 219

Smalltalk Best Practice Patterns (Beck), 143, 189

Smell of the Week practice exercise, 36

Social Security number, 115, 234

Software, 23, 26, 251–252

Software metric, 41

Software perfection, 17

Sparkline script

  code smells, 5–6

  Comments, 10–11

  consistency, 6–7

  Derived Values, 15–17

  Greedy Methods, 8–9

  Greedy Module, 9–10

  HTTP wrapper, 7–8

  methods, 4, 7–8, 11–13

  Preserve Whole Object, 11–12

  `puts`, 4, 8, 13–15

  `sparky.rb`, 8, 86, 225

  testing, 8, 13

  transforms, 15–16

Special Case, 96–97

Speculative Generality, 68–69, 76–77, 222

SQL, 190, 192–195, 249–250

SQLite, 249

Stack, 197, 201, 209, 221

Street address, 115, 234

String class API, 51–54, 218

String methods, 54, 227

Strings, 81, 178

Structs, 151, 241

`sub`, 227

Subjunctive programming, 179

Substitute Algorithm, 84, 191–194, 227, 229

Substring, 227, 246

Subversion (version control), 177

Superclasses, 63, 85, 154, 221

Sustainable process, 22–23

SVG, 8–10, 15–16

`svg.rb`, 10, 18

Synonyms, 228

System of Names, 136, 165

T

`tagname`, 229

TDD (test-driven development), 19, 22–23, 195

TDD/BDD microprocess, 22

Team/partner assistance, 25, 36, 37–38, 179

Tease Apart Inheritance, 159

Telephone number, 115, 234

Tell, Don't Ask, 143

Template exercise, 88–89

Temporary Field, 114, 146, 237

Test coverage, 188, 248

Test (refactoring micro-process step), 32

Test suite, 25, 28

Testing, 26, 28–30

`Test::Unit`, 26, 28

`text`, 9

Text formatting, 218

Text processing, 218

Thomas, David, 143, 152

Time recording program

  `ActiveRecord`, 194, 249–250

  CSV strings, 190, 248

  hexagonal architecture, 190, 248

  persistence, 189, 194

  rates of change, 189, 248

  script, 183–187

source code, 183 *n*1
substitute algorithm, 191–194,
    248–249
test-driven development, 195
`TimelogFile`, 189–190, 192–193,
    248–249
Tk, 205
`to_f`, 59
`to_i`, 59, 218
Tools for refactoring, 25–26, 229
`to_proc`, 224
`to_s`, 59, 199, 203, 205, 209, 218, 235
`to_xml`, 91, 229
Transforms (SVG), 15–16
Triggers, 55, 220
Type-checking, 211
Type Embedded in Name, 59, 62,
    220–221

U
UI class, 211
UML model, 190
UML sketches, 26
Uncommunicative Name, 5, 14–15, 60, 62,
    175–176, 209, 220–221
Underscores, 209
`unless`, 96
Up-front design, 20
URLs
    calculator program code, 197 *n*1
    code downloads, 18
    game program code, 173 *n*1
    mailing list for this book, 38
    Rcov, 76
    refactoring tools, 251–252

Ruby Application Archive, 228
time program code, 183 *n*1
Utility Function, 5, 138–139, 151, 240–241

V
`variable = value || default`, 94
Variables, 98–99, 103
Variation point, 154, 190, 192, 194, 249
Verbs, 57
Version control, 26, 177
Vocabulary, 57–58, 61

W
Wabi-Sabi, 17
Wabi-Sabi (Koren), 17
Walking a List, 148–149, 239
Whole objects, 11–12, 112
Winner method, 175, 178
Working Effectively with Legacy Code (Feathers),
    26, 241
Wrapper, 164–166, 243
WrappingPoint class, 229

X
`x_axis`, 11–12, 16
XML, 6, 10
XML report, 91–92, 229

Y
`y_values`, 12, 15

Z
ZIP code, 115, 118, 234–235
Zipped documents, 162
Zumbacker Z function, 169, 245

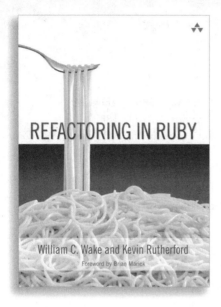

FREE Online Edition

Your purchase of **Refactoring in Ruby** includes access to a free online edition for 45 days through the Safari Books Online subscription service. Nearly every Addison-Wesley Professional book is available online through Safari Books Online, along with more than 5,000 other technical books and videos from publishers such as Cisco Press, Exam Cram, IBM Press, O'Reilly, Prentice Hall, Que, and Sams.

SAFARI BOOKS ONLINE allows you to search for a specific answer, cut and paste code, download chapters, and stay current with emerging technologies.

Activate your FREE Online Edition at
www.informit.com/safarifree

> **STEP 1:** Enter the coupon code: GWKFREH.

> **STEP 2:** New Safari users, complete the brief registration form.
> Safari subscribers, just log in.

If you have difficulty registering on Safari or accessing the online edition, please e-mail customer-service@safaribooksonline.com